Folk Tales of Brittany

FOLK TALES
OF BRITTANY

FOREWORD

These tales are still characteristic of the tales told or sung in the farmhouses, at weddings and christenings in the Breton-speaking regions of Brittany, in spite of the disastrous modern influence of moving pictures and popular songs.

Some of the stories in this book are unpublished hitherto in their present form—the subjects of them being taken from the ancient folk songs of Barzaz-Breize, or from oral tradition. Others are translated from the old collection of legends gathered in the Breton language, from the Breton people, by the distinguished writer and son of Brittany, Emile Souvestre, and published in French under the title of *Le Foyer Breton*.

I wish to express special gratitude to M. l'Abbé François Cadic, who has allowed me the use of his remarkable series of fairy and folk tales *Contes et Légendes de Bretagne* and *Nouveaux Contes et Légendes*, which together with their historical commentary form what Anatole Le Braz justly calls *Le Livre d'Or du Morbihan*.

ELSIE MASSON
Pontivy, Morbihan
France
October, 1929.

CONTENTS

LIST OF ILLUSTRATIONS

THE CASTLE OF COMORRE

Beware, beware, lost creature

LONG ago in the town of Vannes there lived a king who had an only daughter. Her name was Tréphine. She was the loveliest princess in all of Brittany and all the lands that lay beyond. Moreover, she had never committed a mortal sin. And so the king, her father, would rather have lost all his castles, farms, and horses than to have seen Tréphine unhappy.

One day ambassadors came to the King of Vannes from the country of Cornouaille, from Count Comorre, a powerful ruler at that time. They brought with them gifts of honey, linen thread, and a dozen suckling pigs and gave them to the king, telling him that Count Comorre wished to marry the Princess Tréphine. They said that their master had visited the last fair disguised as a soldier, that he had seen the young princess and had fallen in love with her.

The request for her hand caused the princess and her father the deepest grief. For you must know that Comorre was a wicked and mighty tyrant. He loved to do evil. In deed he was so cruel that when he was a mere boy whenever he went forth from the castle his mother used to rush to the alarm bell in the tower and ring it to warn the townsfolk that he was coming. As he grew older he became more wicked every day so that he was feared and hated by all. But worst of all he had already had four wives whom he had killed.

Therefore the King of Vannes told the ambassadors that his daughter was too young to marry. But the Northerners declared roughly, as was their way, that Comorre would not accept any such excuse, and that he had commanded them to declare war on the King of Vannes if permission were not granted to take the princess back to the castle of the Count. Let the king say no at the peril of his crown.

The king was a brave man, and with fury in his heart he declared that Tréphine should not go. Then quickly he gathered together all his soldiers and his knights to defend his country. Thus did he defy the evil Comorre.

Scarcely had three days passed before Count Comorre marched down on Vannes at the head of his mighty army. The king went forth with his array of knights and soldiers to meet him.

Now when Saint Gildas saw these armed hosts making ready for a bloody fray he went to find the princess who was praying in her oratory. The saint was wearing the mantle that he had used as a boat to sail over the sea, and he was carrying the staff that had been the mast. A fiery aureole was glowing around his head.

Gildas entering the oratory petitioned the princess to avert the battle. He said that the men of Brittany were about to fall upon one another's throats and that she could prevent the death of many Christians if she would agree to marry Comorre.

"Alas, why am I not a beggar maid!" exclaimed the princess, wringing her hands. "Then at least I could marry the beggar of my choice! But if I must marry this oppressor then say for me the offices of the dead. I know the Count will slay me as he has slain his other wives."

But Saint Gildas replied, "Fear nothing, Tréphine. Here is a silver ring as white as silk. It will warn you if Comorre plots villainies against you, for it will then turn as black as a raven's wing. Take courage and save the Bretons from death."

And so the young princess consented to marry Comorre.

The saint went at once to the two armies and told them of Tréphine's decision. The king received the news with sorrow. He did not wish to give his consent to the marriage, in spite of his daughter's resolve. But Count Comorre made him so many promises that at last he agreed to accept him as a son-in-law.

The wedding was celebrated with great festivities. The first day six thousand guests were feasted, and the next day as many more, and the newly married couple waited on them at table.

At last when all the soup pots were emptied and the barrels drunk down to the dregs, the guests went home, and Comorre carried off his young bride as a hawk carries off a little white dove.

Now it happened during the next few months his love for Tréphine made Comorre gentler than you would have expected from the wickedness of his nature. The dungeons of the castle were empty and no one was put to death.

"What has happened to our Count that he no longer revels in tears and bloodshed?" many of his unhappy subjects asked each other. But those who knew him better waited and said nothing.

Tréphine was not happy in spite of her husband's kindness. Every day she went to the chapel of the castle and prayed on the tombs of the four wives of whom the Count was widower. She prayed to God to preserve her from death.

At this time there was a gathering from far and wide of Breton princes at Rennes, and Comorre was compelled to go. On his departure he gave the princess all his keys, even the cellar keys, and, telling her to do as she liked, he set out with a retinue of horsemen and men-at-arms.

He did not return for six months, and he came back to the castle eager to see the princess, who during his absence had been constantly in his thoughts. He went quickly to her room and as he entered he saw that she was making a baby's satin hood covered with silver embroidery.

When he beheld her work he grew pale and asked, "For what child are you making that?"

The princess who thought that it would bring him great happiness answered, "In a short time, Count, a child will be born to us."

Not a word said Comorre in reply, but his countenance grew dark with anger and after having darted a terrible look at the princess abruptly left the room.

Tréphine glanced down and noticed that her little silver ring which the saint had given her had turned black. She uttered a cry of terror for she remembered Saint Gildas' words and she knew that grave danger threatened her.

Night was falling and she fled to the chapel. She remained there as the hours tolled crouching by one of the tombs of the dead wives. Midnight struck. As the last note sounded the princess saw four ghostlike figures slowly moving toward her. All but dead with terror she tried to flee, but one of the wraiths addressed her in sepulchral voice:

"Beware, beware, lost creature! Comorre is on the watch to kill you!"

"To kill me!" exclaimed the princess. "What have I done to make him wish me dead?"

"He knows that you will soon be the mother of a child and it has been foretold that his son will be the cause of his destruction," answered the ghostly creature.

"Heaven help me! What can I do to escape from his cruelty?" cried Tréphine, wringing her hands.

"Go back to your father in the land of the white corn," said the spectre.

"But how can I escape?" asked the princess. "Comorre's great dog keeps watch in the courtyard."

"Give the dog the poison that killed me," said the first ghostly wife.

"And how shall I get over the high wall?" asked Tréphine trembling.

"Use the rope that strangled me," replied the second phantom.

"Who will direct me in the darkness?" the princess asked.

The fire that burnt me," the third spectre answered.

How shall I walk so far?" asked poor Tréphine with anguish in her heart.

"Take this staff that cleft my brow," said the last ghostly wife.

The princess took the staff, the fire, the rope, and the poison, and thanking the ghostly shades she fled in haste. She prevented the dog from attacking her, she got over the great wall, the fire lighted her in the darkness, and leaning on the staff she took the road to Vannes where lived the king, her father.

When the wicked Comorre could not find the princess the next morning he sent searchers throughout the castle. All came back reporting that no trace of the princess could be found.

Then Comorre climbed to the top of the lofty central tower and looked toward the four winds. Toward the midnight he saw a raven croaking, toward the sunrise he saw a swallow flying, toward the midday a sea-gull hovering, but toward the sunset he saw a white dove fleeing.

"That is Tréphine," he said to himself.

And he saddled his horse and set out in pursuit.

The princess by this time was on the outskirts of the forest which surrounded the castle of Comorre, but she was warned of his approach for she saw her ring again turn black. She ran across a heath and reached a shepherd's hut where there was no one but an old magpie in the cage.

There the princess lay all day in hiding. But when night fell she continued on her way by paths that ran along the flax fields, guided by the fire and supported by the staff.

For two days Comorre did not find her, then he turned back through the heath. There, alas, he found the shepherd's hut and heard the magpie imitating the princess' moans and crying in its rasping voice, "Poor Tréphine, O Poor Tréphine!"

So Comorre knew at once that the princess had passed that way. He called his hound and put him on the scent, then leaped upon his steed and followed.

In the meantime, the princess, winged by fear, was fleeing. She was near Vannes and her father's castle. She came to a bosky wood and feeling she could go no farther she stopped to rest. And there in the glade a beautiful child was born to her. It was he who later became the great king and saint, Trémeur.

As the princess clasped the child in her arms she saw a falcon on a nearby tree. On his foot was a golden ring, which she recognized as belonging to her father. She called the falcon by name and he flew down onto her lap. Then she gave him the saint's silver ring.

"Falcon," she said, "fly to my father and give him this ring. When he sees it he will know I am in grave danger, and you must direct him and his soldiers how to come to me."

The bird understood, took the ring, and flew away to Vannes.

But at this very moment Comorre appeared on the road with his hound which was following Tréphine's scent. Poor Tréphine! She had given her ring to the falcon and she was not warned of Comorre's approach until she heard the tyrant's voice urging on the dog.

Quickly the princess wrapped the child in her cloak and hid him in the hollow of a tree. Barely had she done so when Comorre on his hairy horse rode up beside her.

When he saw Tréphine he uttered a wild cry and drawing his cutlass quickly struck off her head. Then satisfied that he had destroyed her he called his hound and cantered back to the castle.

Meantime the falcon had reached the court of the King of Vannes. The king was dining with Saint Gildas. As the falcon flew over the table he let the ring fall into the king's drinking cup. The king took it out and exclaimed:

"Some evil has befallen our daughter, the falcon has brought back her ring. Saddle the horses at once. Let Gildas come with us. I fear we shall need his help."

Quickly the horses were made ready and a great company set out with the king and Saint Gildas to find the princess. They followed the falcon's flight, galloping till they came to the glade where the princess lay dead. There they found her, and her child hidden in the tree.

The king got down from his horse weeping bitterly and all within his retinue were overcome with grief.

But Gildas imposed silence.

"Upon your knees," directed he, "and pray to God with me. The evil may yet be undone." So saying he knelt with all there present and after having uttered fervent prayer he addressed the princess. "Rise up," commanded he.

And Tréphine obeyed and taking her head the saint set it on her shoulders and she was alive again.

"Take thy child," again the saint directed, "and come with us to the castle of Comorre."

And the princess did as the saint had bidden and with the king and his terrified attendants sped swiftly to the castle of the Count. But however swift the horses sped the princess carrying her son was swifter. Thus they reached the stronghold of Comorre.

Comorre beheld them coming from afar and hastened to pull up the drawbridge. And when Saint Gildas and the princess drew near the moat the saint cried in a loud voice:

"Comorre! Comorre! I am bringing back your wife alive, and behold your son as God gave him unto you! Will you take them under your roof?"

Gildas repeated the same words twice, then thrice, but no voice answered. He took the baby from his mother's arms and placed him standing on the ground. Then lo! A miracle was seen. The child walked to the brink of the moat, and stooping took a handful of sand and threw it against the castle walls. Lifting his arms toward Heaven he called out in a ringing voice:

"Justice shall be done!"

Immediately the towers of the castle fell over with the noise of thunder, the walls split open and in an instant all the mighty stronghold of Comorre toppled into ruin, burying the tyrant and all his wicked followers beneath the stones.

Then the king took the princess and her son and with Gildas and all that great company returned to Vannes, rejoicing.

THE BASIN OF GOLD AND
THE DIAMOND LANCE

The Enchanted Forest

THERE once lived near the town of Vannes an orphan boy named Peronnik. When he was hungry he asked the farm women of the countryside for their broken bread. When he was thirsty he drank at springs, and when he was sleepy he sought out a haystack and curled himself within its shade. Peronnik was a happy lad, however, for whenever he had the wherewithal to ease his hunger he sang with a voice as sweet as an angel's, and thanked God for having given him so many blessings.

One day Peronnik came to a farmhouse built on the edge of a forest, and as he was well-nigh famished he went to the door and asked for a crust of bread. The farmer's wife was scraping out the porridge pot with a flint, but when she heard Peronnik's voice she gave him the pot to finish. He sat down on the doorstep and putting the saucepan between his knees began to scrape away with a will.

"This is oatmeal fit for a king," he exclaimed 'twixt ravenous mouthfuls.

The farmer's wife was delighted at the praise of her porridge.

"Poor lone boy," she said, "there is not much left, but I will give you some homemade bread."

She brought the lad a small loaf fresh from the oven, and he bit into it like a wolf, declaring that it must have been kneaded by the baker of My Lord Bishop of Vannes.

The peasant woman, bursting with pride to hear her bread so applauded, said it was much better with butter. And she brought Peronnik a pot of butter freshly churned.

Peronnik spread it on the bread, declaring there was no butter like it in all the land of Brittany, and the dame was so delighted that she gave him a bit of last Sunday's bacon. The boy swallowed it as if it had been spring water, for it had been many a long day since he had been so bounteously fed.

While Peronnik was enjoying himself thus a knight came riding by and asked the farmwife the way to the Castle of Kerglas.

"Blessings on us! Can it be that you are going there?" asked the woman in astonishment.

"Yes," replied the knight, "and to go to the Castle of Kerglas I have come from a country so far away that I have been travelling day and night for many moons."

"And what do you seek at Kerglas?" the dame inquired.

22

"I am seeking the golden basin and the diamond lance," the stranger answered.

"Are they very valuable?" asked Peronnik, who had been listening with both ears.

"They are worth more than all the kings' crowns in the world," replied the knight. "For not only does the golden basin give you all the food you may desire, but if you drink from it you will be cured of any sickness. As for the diamond lance it will destroy all that it strikes."

"And who has this basin of gold and this diamond lance?" asked Peronnik amazed.

"They belong to a wizard named Rogéar. He is a giant who lives in the Castle of Kerglas," interrupted the farmer's wife who had heard of the wizard before. "You may oft see him ride near the edge of the forest," she continued. "He mounts a black mare who is followed by her foal. But no one dares attack the wizard for he carries the magic lance."

"Yet I am told he does not bear it in the castle," said the knight. "Rogéar locks his lance and his basin in a dark keep beneath the ground. I plan to attack the wizard and win his magic treasures."

"You will never succeed, good Sir Knight," said the farm woman. "More than a hundred noblemen have tried this adventure but not one has ever returned."

"I know that full well, worthy dame," answered the knight, "but I have had instructions from the hermit of Polavet."

"What did the hermit tell you?" asked Peronnik eagerly.

"He warned me that I must pass through a wood where magic spells await me and where I may lose my way," the knight replied. "If I succeed in passing through the wood I shall meet an elf armed with a fiery dart. This elf is guarding an apple tree from which I must pick an apple."

"And after that?" queried Peronnik.

"I must find the flower that laughs," the knight continued. "It is guarded by a lion whose mane is formed of vipers. But I must pluck the flower. Then I shall have to cross the dragon's lake and fight the blackamoor. He is armed with an iron ball which always hits its mark and then returns to its master."

"Is that all?" Peronnik asked.

"No," answered the knight, "for finally I must go through the Valley of Delights where I shall see everything that can tempt and hold me back. Then when I pass the valley I shall come to a river with a single ford. There shall I find a lady draped in black. I must carry her across the river and she will tell me what next is to be done that I may gain my quest."

The farmer's wife tried to persuade the knight not to undertake the venture. She felt assured no man successfully could undergo all these dire ordeals.

"This is not a matter that a woman can judge," announced the strange knight haughtily, and after the entrance to the forest had been pointed out to him he spurred his horse and disappeared among the trees. The woman sighed, declaring that there would soon be another soul before the judgment Throne.

Peronnik was about to go upon his way when the farmer arrived from the fields. He was in need of a cowherd and he had no sooner seen Peronnik than he decided to engage him.

Peronnik was delighted to enter the farmer's service because of the good food he knew the farmer's wife would give him. So out to field on the edge of the forest went the boy to watch the cows and to bring them home at sunset.

One day shortly after this as he was running to and fro among the cows Peronnik heard the sound of horses' hoofs, and looking toward the forest he saw the giant Rogéar riding his black mare followed by her foal.

On a cord around the giant's neck hung the golden basin and in his hand he bore the diamond lance. Peronnik, frightened, hid behind a bush until the giant had passed by and had disappeared among the trees.

Almost daily several times after this the wizard Rogéar rode past Peronnik, until the boy at length quite used to seeing him, ran to hiding no longer. Peronnik was thinking how much he himself wished to follow the adventure, of which the knight had told. "And what a glorious thing it would be," he mused, "to get possession of the golden basin and the diamond lance!"

One afternoon when Peronnik was alone in the meadow watching the cattle he saw a man with a flowing beard standing at the edge of the forest. Peronnik wondered whether he were a stranger come as had the knight to seek his fortune, so approaching the bearded figure he asked him if he were looking for the road to the Castle of Kerglas.

"No, I am not looking for it," answered the stranger through his beard, "for I already know it."

"You have been to Kerglas and the giant did not kill you!" exclaimed Peronnik.

"Rogéar has nothing to fear from me," the white-bearded man replied. "I am the sorcerer Bryak, Rogéar's elder brother. When I wish to see him I come here, and as I cannot go through the enchanted wood without being lost, in spite of my magic power, I call the black colt to show me the way."

As he spoke he stooped over and drew three circles in the dust, muttering magic words, then cried aloud:

"Foal, free of foot,
Foal, free of tongue,
    Foal, here am I.
Come to me, O come,
Free of foot and tongue,
    Foal, here wait I."

The little horse appeared at once. Bryak put a bridle on him, swung upon his back and disappeared into the forest.

Peronnik said nothing of this to anyone, but now he understood the first thing necessary to get to the Castle of Kerglas was to ride the colt who knew the way. The boy did not know how to draw the magic circles, nor how to say the magic words, but he did remember the verse to call the colt. Nor yet knew he the proper way to gather the apple, to pluck the flower that laughs, to escape from the blackamoor's ball, or to go through the Valley of Delights.

Peronnik decided to make a bridle of flax, a snare to catch snipe which he dipped in holy water, and a linen bag which he filled with glue and larks' feathers. Then he took his rosary, a wooden whistle, and a bit of bread rubbed with rancid bacon. With these things Peronnik was ready to begin the adventure.

The next morning he took the bread the farmer's wife had given him and crumbled it along the path that the giant Rogéar would be sure to follow. And in a short time Rogéar on the horse followed by the colt came out of the woods and crossed the meadow just as he had done before. But this time the colt, smelling the bread, sniffled the ground. He then stopped and ate the crumbs and thus was soon left alone, as the giant on horseback passed quickly on among the trees.

Then Peronnik sang in his clear voice:

> "Foal, free of foot,
> Foal, free of tongue,
> Foal, here am I.
> Come to me, O come,
> Free of foot and tongue,
> Foal, here wait I."

The foal stopped, turned, and quickly came to Peronnik, who gently bridled him. The lad then jumped upon his back and gave the colt his head, for he was sure the colt knew the way to Kerglas. And indeed the colt without the slightest hesitation took one of the wildest paths into the forest and trotted quickly into its gloomy depths.

The ride was terrible to Peronnik and he trembled with fear. The forest was enchanted. and spells were cast to terrify him. The trees appeared to be in flames; they loomed appallingly, like specters of some nether world; the streams became enraged torrents., and overhanging rocks seemed threatening to topple. Peronnik pulled his cap over his eyes so he could not see what dread shapes surrounded him, and the colt bounded ever forward.

At last they came out of the forest to a plain where the spells were ended. Peronnik now dared to look about him. It was a desolate spot and here and there were skeletons of nobles who had come to seek the Castle of Kerglas.

Peronnik, shuddering, passed quickly onward and came at length to a meadow which was shaded by a mighty apple tree that groaned beneath its load of fruit. Near the tree stood an elf and in his hand was the fiery dart that turns all that it may touch to ashes.

When the elf saw Peronnik he uttered a loud cry and instantly raised the dart. But Peronnik, without appearing at all to look surprised, took his cap in his hand and said politely:

"Do not bother about me, little prince, I am going through the meadow only to reach Kerglas."

"And who are you?" demanded the elf, lowering his arm.

"I am Peronnik, you know," answered the boy.

"I know nothing of the kind," retorted the elf.

"I pray you to not let me waste my time," said Peronnik.

"I have the wizard's colt and I must take it on to Kerglas."

The elf seeing that he indeed did have the colt was about to let him pass when he noticed the snare Peronnik was carrying.

"For what is that?" asked he.

"That is to catch birds," Peronnik replied. "No thing that flies can escape its meshes."

"I should like to be assured of that," said the elf. "My apple tree is plundered by the blackbirds. Get your snare ready and if you catch a blackbird I will agree to let you pass."

Peronnik accepted the proposal. He tied the colt to a branch, then went to the trunk of the tree, fixed one end of the snare to it and asked the elf to hold the other end while he prepared the pegs. The elf did so. Then Peronnik deftly tightened the slipknot, and in a trice the dwarf found himself captured in the snare.

The elf uttered a howl of rage and fought to free himself, but the cord which had been dipped in holy water held ever tightly. Peronnik then picked an apple from the tree, mounted once more upon the back of the foal and rode off while the elf still raged within the captive meshes.

Peronnik soon left the plain behind him and came to a lovely glade where grew sweet shrubs and plants of every known delicious fragrance. In the midst of all, there nodded the mysterious laughing flower. But a lion was guarding this glade. He had a mane of vipers, and his growl resounded like the rumblings of thunder. Woe to that adventurer who fell within his claws!

Peronnik took off his cap to the lion and wished him good luck, and then asked if this were the right road to Kerglas.

"And what business have you at Kerglas?" roared the lion, fire flashing from his eyes.

"I am returning the wizard's colt, do you not see?" Peronnik asked in return.

Well, yes, the lion did see it.

"But before I let you pass, reveal the contents of your bag," commanded the mighty beast approaching Peronnik and sniffing the sack which held the feathers and the glue.

"I shall be glad to," said the boy, "but beware, for what is in it might fly out."

"Birds! Open it a little then, and let me look in," growled the beast who by now had become very curious indeed.

That was just what Peronnik wanted, so he held out the bag half opened and the lion plunged in his head. Of course the feathers and the glue stuck to him. Peronnik quickly pulled the string and fastened it tightly around the lion's neck. Then he rushed toward the laughing flower, plucked it and rode off as swiftly as the colt could carry him.

Riding thus it did not take long to reach the lake of the twelve dragons. Across this the lad had to swim upon the colt, and hardly had they touched the water than the dragons came crowding to devour him.

This time Peronnik did not trouble to take off his cap. He began at once to throw the beads of his rosary to the dragons who snapped at them as if they had been cherries. As each dragon swallowed a bead he rolled over on his back and died. Thus Peronnik and the colt swam safely to the far side of the lake.

But Peronnik had yet to enter the valley watched over by the blackamoor, and before long he beheld this evil man in the narrow entrance to the valley. He was chained to a rock by one foot and he had in his hand the iron ball which always hit that at which it was thrown and then returned to its master. This blackamoor had six eyes around his head and each eye took its turn awatching while the others slept. At this moment all six eyes were open.

Peronnik knew that if the blackamoor saw him he would hurl the iron ball and it would crush him. So Peronnik dodged among the woods, and in this way managed to get quite close to the blackamoor who had just sat down to rest and had closed two of his eyes.

Encouraged by this Peronnik began to sing in his soft and musical voice and the blackamoor shut his third and fourth eyes. Peronnik sang on and the Blackamoor slowly closed his fifth eye. The lad then began to chant the vespers and before he had finished the blackamoor was fast asleep.

The lad now took the colt by the bridle and led him noiselessly over the grass-grown road. He passed the blackamoor without a sound and entered at length the Valley of Delight.

This valley resembled a lush garden with blossoms, fruit trees, and sparkling fountains. The fountains played wine instead of water, the flowers sang and the trees reached down their branches and offered their bounteous harvest. Peronnik saw tables spread as for a king. He smelled the delicious odor of fresh cakes and other good things. Servants waited for his commands. Beautiful maidens danced upon the flower-spangled lawns. They called to him by name and invited him to join the revelry.

Peronnik had all but alighted from the colt and at once all would have been over with him when suddenly the memory of the golden basin and the diamond lance bade him pause.

He straightway pulled out his wooden whistle and began to pipe upon it so as not to hear the sweet voices of the maidens. And he ate his bread and rancid bacon and he no longer smelled the enticing spread upon the tables. He fixed his eyes on the colt's ears and so could not see the lovely dancers.

In this way he proceeded through the valley without any mishap and at last in the distance beheld the Castle of Kerglas. But he was cut off from it by the river with one ford. The colt knew well the ford and going directly to it strode out into the water.

Then Peronnik looked about him to find the lady who was to take him to the castle, and there she was seated on a rock. She was dressed in black satin and her face was as dark as the shadows of night.

Peronnik pulled in the colt, and taking off his cap, bowed to the lady.

"I have been waiting for you," she said.

"Will you tell me what next to do?" Peronnik asked.

"Yes," replied the dark lady, "if you will take me across the river."

Peronnik helped her to mount behind him, then continued to ford the river.

"Listen," said she of the satin dress. "The apple tree which was guarded by the elf is a magic tree, and if you can persuade the giant Rogéar to eat the apple which you have brought you may win the golden basin and the diamond lance."

"I shall try," said Peronnik, "and if I succeed how can I obtain the basin and the lance? Are they not hidden in a dark underground chamber which no key can open?"

"The flower that laughs," answered she of the dark countenance, "opens every door and lights the darkest places."

Talking thus they reached the farthest bank and Peronnik, dismounting from the colt, walked toward the castle. Before the entrance gate sat the giant smoking a pipe of pure gold. When he saw Peronnik alighting from the foal he shouted in a voice like thunder:

"By all the magic powers! That is my colt the young scapegrace is riding!"

"Yes, it is, greatest of all magicians," said Peronnik, bowing and taking off his cap.

"And how did you lay hands on it?" the giant Rogéar roared.

"I repeated what I learned from the sorcerer Bryak, your brother," returned Peronnik.

"Foal, free of foot,
Foal, free of tongue,
    Foal, here am I.
Come to me, O come,
Free of foot and tongue,
    Foal, here wait I."

"Humph! And what do you want?" demanded the giant.

"I have brought you two rare gifts from your brother Bryak," Peronnik said, "this dark lady for a serving maid, and this magic apple which will make glad your heart."

"So be it, then, give me the apple," said the giant, "and help the lady to dismount."

31

Peronnik obeyed, and Rogéar took the apple. But no sooner had he bitten into it than from being a mighty giant he turned suddenly into a dwarf so small that he did not reach the top of Peronnik's shoe. Seizing the tiny creature Peronnik popped him into a bird cage and there he could do no mischief. The lad then entered the castle, holding the laughing flower. He passed through fifty rooms and one and came at last to a silver door. This room led to the underground chamber. The door was locked with a ponderous lock, but yielding to the laughing flower it swung open. Peronnik still holding the flower before him entered and beheld awaiting him the golden basin and the diamond lance.

Hardly had Peronnik seized them than the earth began to quake. Thunder rolled and lightning flared, and suddenly the castle vanished and Peronnik found himself at home once more in the field among the cows. But in his hands he clasped the golden basin and the diamond lance.

Carrying these treasures that he had at last won from the Castle of Kerglas, Peronnik set out for the court of the King of Brittany. When he came to the city of Nantes he found it besieged by the French. The French soldiers had so devastated the country around about that there was nothing left but shrubs for the goats to nibble. The people were starving and the soldiers of Brittany who had not died of wounds were dying of hunger.

Now the very day that Peronnik reached Nantes a herald was proclaiming that the King of Brittany would adopt as his heir the man who would deliver the city from the French.

When Peronnik heard this he said to the herald:

"Read your proclamation no more. Take me to the king for I am he whom he seeks."

So when Peronnik came before the king he showed the magic basin and the diamond lance. The king was delighted and promised according to his proclamations to make Peronnik his heir if the lad could free Nantes from the besiegers.

And the king fulfilled his word. For Peronnik by means of the diamond lance quickly swept Brittany of all its enemies. And with the golden basin he restored the wounded Breton soldiers.

It is said that Peronnik went to the Crusades and married a princess of the Saracens. They had many children, to each of whom he gave a kingdom. But others say that the wizard's brother Bryak succeeded in winning back the golden basin and the diamond lance, and that no one now can ever find them no matter where he seeks.

LADY YOLANDA'S THIMBLE

Yolanda's fingers never stopped

Yolanda's fingers never stopped

ALL the warriors of Brittany had gone away to the Crusades. With helmets and spears, and with banners flying, they had set out for the East. They had gone to rescue the Holy Sepulcher from the infidels and to defend it with their lives.

But when the knights and men rode away to the Holy Land they left mourning and sadness behind, for now there would be no more tournaments, no more hunting, no more dancing.

The old men, the women, and the children all asked each other: "When will our warriors come home?"

Season followed season and the knights did not return. Spring took the place of winter, and the country put on its old charm. The birds were singing their joyous love songs, the brooks were babbling gleefully, and the apple trees, dressed in pink and white blossoms, looked like radiant brides. But the men of Brittany remained in the Holy Land.

At last messengers arrived. The Christian army had a heavy task, they said, in its struggle with the infidels and doubtless the war would last for many years to come.

All the country folk at home now fell to work to ease the anguish in their hearts. Never before had Brittany seen such activity. The ladies in the castles were perhaps. the most determined.

They opened their oak chests and brought out silks and brocades, Flanders cloth, and English woolen stuffs, and Italian embroidery. And soon under their fairy-like fingers banners with golden fringes were spread out in the vaulted halls. Scarves were dotted with shining stars, and proud mottoes decorated the walls of the castles. And dainty fingers painted the Mass books with splendid colors. Truly if the knights were doing wonders in the East the ladies in the castles were likewise achieving marvels at home.

Now Old Nick saw this from his dark abode. This change in women's habits did not suit his wicked plans. For their toil and prayers scattered evil thoughts, just as fresh air scatters pestilential odors.

"I must put an end to this," said Old Nick to himself. "And an end there shall be. I am going to cool the zeal of all these busy bees!"

Among Old Nick's followers were all varieties of mischief makers; imps of all sizes and kinds. He thought to himself that he would go to them for advice. He noticed a very fat imp sound asleep in a corner.

"Come, come, Dame Laziness," he shouted, shaking her roughly, "come along with me. I want you to discourage all these mad Breton women who are working so hard that they haven't time for mischief. Go, throw sand into their eyes and make them sleep as soundly as *you* do."

"No, no," answered the lazy imp. "I have already had a try at that, and I didn't succeed a bit. I won't budge now. Let me sleep."

Just then another ugly creature came forward; he was holding a sharp sting in his hand.

"Master," he said, "I will help you. Tonight while all these hard-working ladies are sleeping I will take their needles and dip them in the poison of vipers. That will calm their eagerness. If they prick a finger but once they will cry out so loud that you will hear it down below."

You may be sure the naughty imp spent a busy night. Every needle was poisoned. And what cries and squeaks were heard the next day! Poor dames! The needles would prick in spite of all precautions. In a short time the most eager workers had laid aside their work.

Old Nick was as pleased as pleased can be, and especially so because the women soon began to return to their former habits of indolence. The young ones spent their time on their clothes or admiring themselves in the mirror, when they were not idling on the castle lawns. The older ones gossiped and said unkind things about one another. They all had ceased to think about their men folk fighting in the Holy Land.

But in the midst of all this frivolity and idleness there was one worker who was faithful to her task. That alone was enough to put a drop of bitterness in Old Nick's cup of pleasure.

Yolanda de Tregoët lived in a great castle and there she worked with her needle for the church and for the poor. She was betrothed to a famous knight, Jehan de Kergoff. When the warriors had made ready to depart Yolanda had bade Jehan go, and the young knight at her behest had sewed the Cross upon his tunic.

And now her clever fingers neither stopped nor rested, not even when the needles, by the imp's trick, tortured her and gave her cruel pain. She only laughed at his cunning, while he gnashed his teeth in rage.

"I'll get the better of this minx!" exclaimed Old Nick, angrily.

But Yolanda would not give up her work.

One day Old Nick devised a new plan. He dressed himself like a pilgrim and, staff in hand, looking both poor and devout, he went to ask for charity at Yolanda's castle gate.

He leaned against the arches of the drawbridge and wailed in a doleful voice, "Have pity on a pilgrim from distant lands. A bit of bread, fair damsel!"

Yolanda's kind heart was moved. She ran down quickly to the gate and, taking the pretended pilgrim by the hand, she said, "Come in, come in. Pilgrims are always welcome here; they are heaven-sent."

So Old Nick entered the castle and ate with hearty appetite. He drank still more, for sobriety is not his special virtue. He would have liked to stay longer if a limit were not set to his evil deeds.

When he left he pretended to pay his debt of gratitude to the lady Yolanda. He gave her a shell he had picked up on the seashore, which, he asserted, had touched the Holy Sepulcher and was, in consequence, blessed. In reality he had poisoned the shell.

Yolanda took the shell and kissed it and Old Nick thought that it would cause her destruction. But the deceiver, as so often happens, was deceived in turn. The shell did not hurt her, for no real harm can come to the innocent.

As soon as the pretended pilgrim had gone Yolanda began to sew, but the needle pricked her finger so painfully that she wept in agony. As she wiped the blood away an idea suddenly came to her, she would slip her finger into the shell while she was sewing so as to guard herself from the poisoned needle.

She did so at once and her finger was protected. Not only that, the old wounds were healed, for by a miracle the poison on the shell was turned into a health-giving balm.

Now that very day one of Yolanda's friends came to see her at the castle, and after she had learned of the strange virtue of the shell she thought she too would try it. She knew that the shores of Brittany are dotted over with such shells. They went out on the beach and she and Yolanda hunted until one was found that fitted her exactly. She put it on her finger and it protected her from needle pricks just as did Yolanda's shell.

It was not long, you may be sure, before everyone heard of the discovery. All the women began to pick up shells and to put them on their fingers, and then they set to work again. They sewed and sewed without so much as shedding a single drop of blood.

Farewell now to frivolous amusements, idling, and fine clothes! All the castles in the dukedom were like busy hives, and all of Old Nick's wiles were powerless. For in trying to poison a charitable girl for her industry he had succeeded only in making a present to all women of a convenient tool, the thimble. For in this manner was the thimble brought into being.

The old tool was rough enough at first but soon elaborate ones were made of gold, silver, ivory, or copper, fashioned f or any finger.

As a sign of gratitude Yolanda, who on the return of her lover from the Holy Land became Lady Kergoff, put a thimble among her daughter's wedding gifts, and had a thimble engraved on her armorial bearings.

But in the Breton countryside old grannies may be found who bear a grudge against the thimble. It came, they remember, from Old Nick, and in consequence they remain to. this day faithful to the distaff and the spinning-wheel.

THE WITCH OF LOK ISLAND

Coral ornaments were in her hair

IN olden times when miracles were common in Brittany there lived in Lannilis a youth called Houarn Pogam and a maiden whose name was Bella Postik. They had grown up together and loved each other with all their hearts. When their parents had died, leaving them next to nothing, they were obliged to go into service in the same house.

They ought to have been happy, but lovers are like the ever moaning sea.

"If only we had the means to buy a little cow and a lean pig," said Houarn, "I would hire a bit of land from our master. Then the priest would marry us and we could live together."

"Yes," replied Bella with a heavy sigh, "times are so hard. Cows and pigs were dearer than ever last week at the fair. It is certain that Providence does not care how the world goes round nowadays."

They complained thus every day until at last Houarn became impatient. One morning he went to the threshing-floor where Bella was winnowing grain and told her he was going to set out to seek his fortune.

Bella was very sad on hearing the news and tried to persuade him not to go. But he would not listen.

"Birds fly straight to the corn field," said he, "and bees to the flowers for their honey. A man ought to have as much sense as winged creatures. I am going to find what I want, the price of a little cow and a lean pig. If you love me Bella you will not stand in the way of a plan that will bring about our marriage."

The girl realized that she must consent and said: "Go with Heaven's help, if you must, but before you go I want to give you the most precious treasures my parents left to me."

She led Houarn to her linen press and from it took a little bell, a knife, and a stick.

"These relics have never gone out of our family," she said. "The sound of this bell can be heard at any distance. It warns our friends of any danger we may be in. Whatever this knife touches will escape from the spell of magician or of witch. And lastly this staff will guide the bearer to wherever he may wish to go. I give you the knife to defend you from evil spells, the bell so that it may warn me when you are in danger, but I shall keep the staff and then I shall be able to reach you if you need me."

Houarn thanked his sweetheart. They shed a few tears together, as in duty bound when one says good-bye, and he started off toward the mountains. Then he decided to turn south and after several days reached the town of Pont-Aven.

One morning he was sitting at the door of the inn and saw two salt dealers pass, leading their mules. Houarn overheard their words, and discovered that they were talking about the witch of Lok Island. Houarn went to them and asked what they meant, and they answered that the witch of Lok Island was a fairy who lived in a lake in the biggest of the Glénan Islands. They told Houarn that this witch was richer than all the wealth of the kings of the world. Many a rash lad in search of fortune had gone to the island to find her treasure but not one of them had ever returned.

When Houarn heard this he at once became eager to go to the island to seek adventure. The mule-drivers tried to dissuade him, saying that good Christians like themselves could not see a man go to certain rack and ruin, and they threatened to keep him back by force.

Houarn thanked them for the interest they showed in him and said he was ready to give up the plan if they would pass the hat around and collect enough money for him to buy a little cow and a lean pig. Whereupon they all changed their tune saying that Houarn was a stubborn-headed chap and that they could not stop him anyhow.

So Houarn went down to the seashore and hailed a ferryman who took him over to Lok Island.

He soon found the pool in the middle of the island. It was surrounded with sea-drift covered with pale pink blossoms. Houarn noticed at the far end of the lake in the shade of a clump of flowering broom a sea-green boat floating on the still water. The boat looked like a sleeping swan with its head under its wing.

As Houarn had never seen anything like this he drew near out of curiosity. Then he stepped into the boat to examine it more closely. Hardly had he put his foot in it than the swan awoke. Its head came out from under its feathers, its web feet spread out in the water, and suddenly it left the shore.

The youth uttered a cry of dismay but the swan only floated more quickly toward the middle of the lake. Then the bird put its bill in the water and plunged, carrying Houarn into the depths. In a moment they had reached the witch's home.

It was a palace made of sea-shells, lovelier than anything you can imagine. A crystal stairway led up to the door, and it was built in such a curious way that at each step you took the stair sang like a forest bird. All around the palace were immense gardens and lawns of seaweed set with diamonds instead of flowers, and surrounding the gardens was a forest of sea trees.

Houarn stood in the doorway of the palace, and there in the first room he saw the witch lying on a golden bed. She was dressed in sea-green silk as fine and soft as a wave. Coral ornaments were in her black hair which fell down to her feet. Her pink and white face was as delicately tinted as the inside of a shell.

Houarn drew back at the sight of so delightful a being. But the fairy rose up smiling and went toward him. Her walk was as lithesome as the sweep of the waves on the rolling sea.

"Welcome," she said, motioning him to come in. "There is always a place here for strangers and handsome youths like you."

Houarn felt bolder and entered the room.

"Who are you? Where do you come from? And what do you want?" asked the witch.

"My name is Houarn," said the boy, "I come from Lannilis, and I am looking for enough money to buy a little cow and a lean pig."

"Very well," answered the witch, "your search shall be rewarded,— you shall have your heart's desire."

She then ushered him into a second room the walls of which were hung with threaded pearls. She gave him eight kinds of wine in eight goblets of chased gold. Houarn began by drinking the eight kinds of wine and, as he found them very nice, he drank eight times of each, and always he imagined the witch was more and still more beautiful. Had the world ever seen so enchanting a being?

She told him that the pool of Lok Island was connected by an underground passage with the sea, and that all the wealth of wrecked ships was drawn thither by a magic current.

"On my honor!" cried Houarn whom the wine had made jolly, "I am not surprised that landlubbers speak so badly of you. People as rich as you are always making others envious. As far as I am concerned half your fortune would do for me."

"You shall have it, Houarn," said the witch.

"But how can you manage that?" asked Houarn surprised.

"I have lost my husband who was an elf," she answered; "and so if I am to your taste I will be your wife."

The young man was quite breathless at what he heard. Was it possible that he was to marry the beautiful fairy whose palace was rich enough to contain eight barrels of marvelous wine? To be sure he had promised to marry Bella but memories of Bella were fast becoming clouded by fumes from the witch's brews.

Houarn told the fairy very politely that he could not refuse her offer, and that he was overcome with joy at the prospect of becoming her husband.

The witch then said she would prepare the feast for the betrothal at once. She set a table and spread it with the nicest dishes Houarn had ever set eyes upon, as well as many he had never tasted before. Then she went out into the garden to a fish pond and, taking a net in her hand, leaned out over the water.

"Come hither, come hither, attorney general," she cried. "Come hither, come hither, O, miller! O, tailor! O, beadle!"

Each time she spoke Houarn could see a fish leap into her net.

When the net was full she went back into the palace to the room next to the one where the table was set, and taking a golden frying pan she threw all the fishes into it.

It seemed to Houarn that amidst the sputter of the frying he could hear whispers.

"Who is whispering in your golden frying pan, fairy?" he asked.

"It is just the sparks that the wood is throwing out," she said, blowing up the fire.

But in a moment little voices began to mutter.

"Who is muttering?" asked the young man.

"It is the fat that is melting," she replied, tossing up the fish in the pan.

Soon the voices began to shout.

"Who is shouting so, fairy?" asked Houarn.

"It is only the cricket on the hearthstone," answered the witch, singing so loudly that Houarn could hear nothing else.

Now all that was happening began to clear Houarn's wits. And as he was beginning to be frightened he felt pangs also of remorse.

Mercy on us!" he said to himself, "is it possible that I could forget Bella so soon for a witch who must be the daughter of Old Nick himself? With a wife like that I shall never dare to say my prayers at night. And I shall lose my soul as surely as a pigs' doctor."

Whilst he was thinking thus the witch brought in the fried fish and begged him to sit down to dinner. Then she said she would fetch yet twelve new kinds of wine for him to taste.

Houarn sat down and taking from his pocket the knife Bella had given him, he sighed. Then he tried to eat. But hardly had the spell-destroying knife touched the golden dish than all the fishes stood up and became little men. Each one wore the garb of his profession or trade. There was an attorney general with his white bib, a tailor in violet stockings, a miller all covered with flour, and a beadle in his surplice. And they all shouted out together as they swam in the hot fat:

"Houarn, save us if you wish to be saved yourself."

"Holy saints! Who are all these little men singing in the melted butter?" cried Houarn dumfounded.

"We are Christians like yourself," they shouted back. "We too came to Lok Island to seek our fortune. We agreed to marry the witch, and the day after the wedding she treated us just as she had treated those who came before us, and who are now in the big fish pond."

"Really!" exclaimed Houarn. "Can a woman who seems so young be the widow of all these fishes!"

"And soon you will be in the same state, perhaps fried and eaten by the new comers!" they cried back in a chorus of shrill prophesying voices.

Houarn leaped up as though already he felt himself in the golden frying pan. He rushed toward the door hoping to escape before the witch came back. But she had just slipped in and heard everything. Before Houarn could reach the door she had thrown her steel net over him, and immediately poor Houarn was turned into a frog. Then the witch threw him into the fish pond with her other enchanted husbands.

At that very moment the little bell that Houarn wore, around his neck gave forth a silvery note which Bella heard at far-away Lannilis, where she was busy skimming yesterday's milk.

She uttered a cry, "Houarn is in danger!" And with no more ado, without asking anyone's advice she hurried to her room and put on her Sunday dress, her shoes, and her silver cross. Then, taking the magic staff she left the farm. When she reached the crossroad she stuck her staff in the ground and murmured:

"O, staff of apple wood so fair,
Lead me on land and through the air,
Above the cliffs and o'er the sea,
For with my lover I must be."

The staff changed at once into a chestnut steed, completely saddled and bridled. He had a ribbon above each ear and a blue tassel on his forehead.

Bella mounted and off they started, first at a pace, then at a trot, and then at a gallop. At last they were traveling so swiftly that the trees and the ditches and the church steeples flew past the girl's eyes very much as fly the shuttles of a wool winder.

Yet longed she ever for more speed, and she urged her horse onward, whispering in his ear:

"The horse is less swift than the swallow, the swallow less swift than the wind, the wind is less swift than the lightning, but, steed of mine, you must be swifter than all, for part of my heart is suffering, the dearest half of my heart is in danger."

The horse understood her, and flew like chaff blown before the gale. At last they reached the foot of that rock in the mountains that people call Hart's Leap Rock.

There the swift steed came to a halt for neither man nor beast has eve r climbed that cloud-capped rock. Bella then repeated:

> "O, staff of apple wood so fair,
> Lead me on land and through the air,
> Above the cliffs and o'er the sea,
> For with my lover I must be."

Hardly had she finished the last line when wings grew out of the horse's flanks, and he became a mighty bird that bore her on the winds to the very summit of the cliff .

Here Bella found a nest made of potter's clay, lined with dry moss. On it was sitting a hobgoblin, withered and bearded and dark. He shouted out when he saw Bella:

"Here is the fair maid who has come to save me!"

"To save you!" cried Bella. "Who are you?"

"I am Jennik, the husband of the witch of Lok Island. She it is who with her spells confines me here."

"But what are you doing on that nest?" asked Bella.

"I am trying to hatch six stone eggs, and I shall not get my freedom until they are hatched," answered the hobgoblin.

"Alas, poor little cockerel!" exclaimed the maiden. "How can I deliver you?"

"Just as you will deliver Houarn who is in the witch's power," the elf replied.

"Ah, tell me what I must do!" cried Bella. "Even if I have to go round the four bishoprics, on my bended knees, I shall begin at once."

"Then attend to what I say," continued the goblin.

You must go to the witch of Lok Island and introduce yourself as a young lad. Then you will be on the lookout for your chance to snatch the steel net she carries in her belt. Shut her in it and she will remain there till the judgment Day."

"Where can I get boys' clothes to fit me, little pixie? asked Bella.

"You will soon see, pretty maid."

As he spoke the dwarf pulled out four of his red hairs, blew upon them and muttered beneath his breath. Instantly the four hairs became four tailors. The first tailor held a cabbage in his hand, the second a pair of scissors, the third a needle, and the fourth a flatiron.

Without more ado they sat themselves around the nest with their legs crossed and began to make a young lad's suit for Bella. With the first cabbage leaf they made a fine laced coat. Another leaf soon became the waistcoat, and it took two leaves to make the baggy knickerbockers. Finally a hat was cut out of the heart of the cabbage and the stalk was used to make the shoes.

When Bella had put on these clothes she looked like a young nobleman for her garments were of green velvet, lined with white satin.

"Haste! haste!" cried the pixie when he saw her ready for her adventure. "Away to rescue Houarn!" Bella quickly mounted her great bird and in one flight he transported her to Lok Island. Safely there she ordered him to become again the staff of apple wood. Then getting into the swan boat she plunged downward to the witch's palace just as Houarn had done.

At the sight of the velvet-clad youth the witch was delighted.

"By Old Nick, my first cousin!" she said to herself, "this is the handsomest lad that ever I saw, and I think I shall love him for some time."

So she was all graciousness at once, calling Bella her beloved. Then they went to a table beautifully set with all manner of good things. And there before her Bella saw the magic knife that she had given Houarn and that he had left behind him as he had leaped toward the door.

Bella quickly took the knife and hid it in her pocket. Then, after having partaken of the good things, she followed the witch into the garden. The enchantress showed her the lawns set with diamonds, the fountains with their lavender-scented sprays, and last of all the fish pond where thousands of many-colored fish were swimming. Bella appeared delighted and gazed with rapture upon the gaily colored scales and tails.

The witch seeing her so pleased at once asked her if she would not be glad to live always in the palace.

"Will you consent to marry me?" asked the wicked fairy.

"Oh, yes indeed!" replied Bella, "but first let me try to catch one of those pretty fishes with the steel net you have at your belt."

The witch who suspected nothing thought the request a mere whim of boyish fancy and giving Bella the net said smiling:

"Now, fair fisherman, let us see what may be your luck. A rich catch may await you."

"I will catch Old Nick's cousin!" cried Bella, quickly throwing the net over the witch's head. Then she added, "Accursed witch, become in body what you are in heart!"

The witch uttered one terrifying shriek that ended in a moan, for the girl's wish had instantly come true: the beautiful water pixie had become the hideous Queen of the Toadstools.

Bella hastily rolled up the net and threw it into the well, over which she put a stone sealed with the sign of the cross. And this cannot be lifted until the judgment Day.

Then she ran back to the fish pond, but the fish had already left it and were moving toward her like a procession of many-colored monks. They piped out in their tiny voices:

"Here is our lord and master who has delivered us from the steel net and the golden frying pan!"

"And who will give you back your human form," said Bella, taking out the magic knife.

But just as she was about to touch the first fish with the knife, she noticed at her feet a large green frog. It was on its knees sobbing bitterly with its forepaws crossed upon its breast, and on a cord around its neck there hung the magic bell. Bella felt her heart give a sudden bound and she cried:

"Is that you, my little Houarn? Is that you, king of my joys and of my cares?"

"It is I," groaned the frog.

Then Bella touched him with the knife, and immediately Houarn stood before her in his own true form. They kissed each other, laughing and crying alternately.

Bella then touched each of the fish in turn with the magic knife and all of them became what they had been before the witch had changed them.

As Bella was touching the last fish who should arrive but the hobgoblin of Hart's Leap Rock. He was sitting in his nest which now looked like a chariot while six black beetles were pulling it. These had just been hatched out of the stone eggs.

Here I am, fair maid!" the hobgoblin called to Bella. The spell is broken. May heaven shower blessings on thee! You have made a man of a fowl!"

He jumped out of his chariot, and led the lovers to the witch's treasure chest. When they opened it they found that it was full of precious stones!

"Take as many as you like," said the hobgoblin.

So both Bella and Houarn filled their pockets, their hats, their belts, and even their wide knickerbockers. When they had as many gems as they could carry, Bella ordered her staff of apple wood to become a coach large enough to hold all the people she had set free.

And thus they went to Lannilis.

At last their banns were published, and Houarn and Bella were married. But instead of buying a little cow and a lean pig they bought all the fields in the parish and settled down as farmers. And all the people they had brought from Lok Island settled down there, too.

LITTLE WHITE-THORN AND THE TALKING BIRD

Milk flowed like water of a spring

LONG ago when the oak trees used in building the oldest boat at Brest were but acorns, there lived a poor widow whose name was Ninor. Her father was of noble lineage and had a large fortune. When he died he left a manor house, a farm, a mill, and an oven where all the villagers paid for baking their bread. He left, also, twelve horses and twice as many oxen, twelve cows and ten times that number of sheep, without counting the corn and fine linen.

But as she was a widow Ninor's brothers would not let her have her share of the inheritance. Perrik, the eldest, kept the manor, the farm, and the horses. Fanche, the second, took the mill and the cows. The third brother, Riwal, had the oxen, the great oven, and the sheep. So that nothing was left for Ninor but an old ramshackle cottage on the heath where they usually sent sick animals. Alas, that is often the way of the world!

When Ninor was moving her bits of furniture to her poor cottage, Fanche pretended to be sorry for her.

"I am going to behave to you as a brother and a Christian," said he, "I have an old black cow which I have never been able to fatten and which hardly gives enough milk to feed a new born babe. But you may take her with you. White-thorn can keep her on the heath."

White-thorn was the widow's daughter. She was nearly eleven years old and she was so pale that people called her by the name of the white hedge flower.

So Ninor went away with her little, pale daughter, pulling the cow along with a bit of rope. And when they reached the cottage Ninor sent them on the heath together.

Every day and all the day long White-thorn stayed there looking after Blackie the cow. And poor Blackie had a hard enough time finding a little grass between the stones. White-thorn spent her time making crosses out of broom and daisies while she sang a melancholy air.

One day she noticed a bird perched on one of the flowery crosses she had just stuck in the ground. The bird was chirping and shaking its head. He looked at her as if he wanted to speak. The girl was very much surprised. She went nearer to the bird and listened carefully but she could understand nothing.

White-thorn was entranced with the little bird and she watched it so long that night began to fall. She had forgotten about Blackie. At last the bird flew away, and White-thorn following him with her eyes saw that the stars were twinkling in the sky.

Then she looked for Blackie but could not find her. She called, she struck the tufts of broom with her stick, she went down into the hollows where the rain water had formed little pools, but all in vain, Blackie was not to be found. Alack, what could have happened?

The child heard her mother's voice calling as if some misfortune had befallen. Frightened she hurried on, and at the entrance to the field, on the path leading to their cottage, she saw the widow kneeling near Blackie. Poor Blackie! The wolves from the forest had gotten her and nothing was left but her bones and horns.

White-thorn burst into tears and fell on her knees by her mother. "Oh! Why didn't I know that the wolves were coming!" she sobbed. "I would have made the sign of the cross with my little stick, and they would have fled."

The widow at the sight of her daughter's grief tried to comfort her.

"Do not weep for Blackie as if she were a human being, my darling," she said. "Even though the wolves and bad Christians are against us, Heaven will have pity on us. Come, help me to pick up some faggots and let us go home."

White-thorn did as her mother said, but the tears trickled down her pale, wan cheeks.

"Poor Blackie," she said to herself. "She was no trouble to lead about. She ate anything, and she was beginning to get fat."

That evening White-thorn would eat no supper and during the night she awoke again and again thinking that she heard Blackie lowing at the door. She got up before daybreak and ran out into the fields barefoot and in her petticoat.

As she came near the heath she beheld the same bird that she had seen before perched again on the cross of broom. He was singing and seemed to be calling her. But she understood him no better than she had the day before. She was about to run home when she looked down and saw what she thought was a gold coin lying at her feet. She tried to turn it over with her toe, but it was not a coin. It was the magic herb of gold that you can see only at sunrise if you are barefoot and half-dressed, and at the same time the fairies will bestow on you the gift of sight. Alack-a-day, this happens rarely to poor mortals!

Yet so it was with White-thorn. The moment she touched the herb she understood the language of birds.

"White-thorn, I want to do you a good turn," the bird was saying. "White-thorn, listen to me."

"Who are you?" asked White-thorn, very much astonished that she could understand the bird.

"I am Robin Redbreast," said the bird, "and each year I am allowed to make a poor girl rich. This time I have chosen you."

"Oh, Robin, Robin," cried White-thorn, "shall I be rich enough to have a shining silver cross with a shining silver chain to go about my neck? And a pair of wooden shoes for my feet as well?"

"You shall have a golden cross and silken shoon," answered the bird.

"And what must I do to have all that, little bird?" asked White-thorn.

"You must follow me wherever I lead you," Robin said.

"Oh, yes, indeed," said White-thorn.

And so away Robin Redbreast flew and off went Whitethorn after him. She followed him across the fields and through the woods till they came to the dunes just opposite the Seven Isles. There the bird perched upon a blowing bit of bracken.

"Can you see anything below on the beach?" asked Robin.

"Yes," said White-thorn, "I see a pair of wooden shoes made of beechwood that the fire has never scorched, and a staff of holly-wood that no steel can ever cut."

"Put on the wooden shoes, and take the staff," said Robin Redbreast.

"I will," said White-thorn, running down to the beach.

"Now," directed Robin, "you must walk on the sea till you reach the first island, then you must go round it till you come to a rock all hidden beneath the water reeds, and the reeds must be the color of the sea."

"And then what must I do?" asked the little girl.

"You must gather the reeds and make a halter."

"That will be easy enough," said White-thorn.

"Then you must strike the rock with your holly staff. A cow will come forth. Put the halter on her and bring her home to your mother. It will comfort her for having lost Blackie."

White-thorn carried out all the talking bird's instructions. With the magic shoes she walked on the sea to the first island. She went round it till she came to the rock with the sea-green reeds. With these she made a halter, as the bird had directed. Then with her holly staff she struck the rock. Instantly it opened and out of it came a cow just as the bird had said.

The cow's skin was as smooth as a maiden's cheek, her eyes soft as the light of dawn. She was very gentle and White-thorn put the halter on her and led her over the water, and then over the fields, and through the woods, and across the heath till they reached the widow's cottage. And when White-thorn's mother, Ninor, saw the cow she was as happy as she had been sad. But she was still happier when she milked the cow, for the milk flowed between Ninor's fingers like the water of a spring.

Ninor filled all her pots and pans, then she filled her wooden bowls, then her crocks and then her churns, yet still the milk flowed on. It seemed as if beautiful Sea-cow, for that is what the talking bird had named her, had milk for all the babes in Brittany.

Soon everyone was gossiping about the widow's cow, and people came from far and near to look upon her. The richest farmers offered to buy Sea-cow and each offered a higher price than the others.

At last Perrik came and said to his sister, "If you are a Christian you will remember that I am your brother and you will let me have the first offer. Let me have Sea-cow and in exchange I will give you as many of my cows as it takes men to make a tailor."

"Sea-cow is not only worth nine cows," answered the widow Ninor, "she is worth all the cows that are grazing in the highlands and the lowlands. Thanks to her I shall be able to sell milk in all the market places from Dinan to Carhaix."

"Very well," said Perrik, "give her to me, sister, and I will give you our father's farm where you were born with all the fields and ploughs and horses belonging to it."

Ninor accepted Perrik's offer. So they all went to the farm, and, after Ninor had dug up a clump of earth in each field, drunk a cup of water from the well, lighted a fire on the hearth, and cut a tuft of hair from each of the horses' tails to prove she had become the owner of all these things, she gave Sea-cow to her brother Perrik. So Perrik led the cow away to a house he had in another quarter of that country.

Little White-thorn cried when she saw her dear Sea-cow led away, and she was sad all that day. When night fell she went into the stable to put hay in the mangers for the horses. They seemed to look at her with sympathy.

"Alas," she sighed, "why is Sea-cow not here too? When shall I see her again?"

Hardly had she spoken when she heard a gentle lowing, and, as she knew the language of animals, having stepped on the golden herb, she understood these words:

"Little Mistress, here I am again."

Very much astonished, White-thorn turned quickly and at her very shoulders there stood Sea-cow!

"Oh! Sea-cow! Sea-cow!" cried the girl, "who brought you here?"

"I do not belong to your wicked Uncle Perrik," said Sea-cow, "because I cannot belong to anyone who is in a state of mortal sin. I came back to be yours as before."

56

"But then," said little White-thorn, "my mother will have to give back the farmhouse, the fields, and the horses."

"Not at all," answered Sea-cow, "for they were hers by right, her brother took them from her unjustly when your grandfather died."

"But my uncle Perrik will come to look for you here," said White-thorn.

"I will tell you what to do," Sea-cow said: "first go and pick three verbena leaves."

White-thorn ran off and quickly returned with the three leaves.

"Now," said Sea-cow, "rub me with those leaves from my ears to my tail, and whisper softly three times, "Saint Ronan of Hibernia, Saint Ronan of Hibernia, Saint Ronan of Hibernia!"

White-thorn did as she was told and, as she whispered for the third time, Sea-cow turned into a beautiful horse.

The little girl was wonder-struck.

"Now," said the horse, "your Uncle Perrik will not know me. My name is no longer Sea-cow but Sea-horse."

When the widow heard what had happened she was delighted. The very next day she hastened to try her fine new horse. She loaded his back with corn to take to market. But you can imagine her surprise when she saw Sea-horse's back growing longer and longer the more she piled on the sacks of corn. So that he alone could carry as many sacks as all the horses in the parish.

You may be sure that the news of it soon spread abroad. When Fanche heard of it he came to the farm and asked his sister if she would sell him the horse. She refused at first till he proposed to give her in exchange the mill and all the pigs he was fattening. So the bargain was struck. And Ninor took possession of the mill as she had of the farm, and then her brother led Sea-horse away.

The very next evening the horse was home again. And again White-thorn picked three verbena leaves and rubbed him from his ears to his tail repeating the words, "Saint Ronan of Hibernia," three times. No sooner had she done so than the horse changed into a sheep. But instead of white wool he was covered with scarlet wool as long as hemp and as soft as flax. Sea-horse was now Sea-lamb. White-thorn was delighted and called her mother who came into the stable to admire this new miracle.

"Go and fetch the shepherd's shears," she said to Whitethorn, "the poor dear beast is weighted down with such a heavy fleece."

But when she tried to sheer Sea-lamb the wool grew again as fast as she cut it off. So that this sheep alone was worth all the flocks on the mountains.

Now Ninor's third brother, Riwal, happened to be passing by and he saw what was happening. He at once offered to exchange his oxen, his heaths, and all his sheep for Sea-lamb.

So the widow gave Riwal the sheep. But as he was leading Sea-lamb along the shore suddenly she threw herself into the waves. She swam to the smallest of the Seven Isles, the rock opened to let her pass, closed again, and she was gone.

This time White-thorn waited in vain for her to come home. She neither came back that day nor the next day, nor ever again.

So the girl ran off to the hawthorn bush to look for the talking bird, and there he was singing away as before.

"I was expecting you, little lady," said the talking bird. "Sea-lamb has gone and will never return. Your wicked uncles are punished as they deserved, and now you are an heiress. You are rich enough to wear a golden cross and silken shoon as I promised you. Now my work is done and I shall fly away. Always remember that you were once poor and that it was a little wild bird that made you rich."

And so the talking bird spread his wings and vanished from little White-thorn's ken. But out of gratitude she had a church built on the spot where the bird had perched upon the broom, and she always gave to the poor.

PRINCESS AHEZ AND THE LOST CITY

The waves rose swiftly higher

IN olden times there lived, in South Brittany, a powerful king named Grallon. He was an upright ruler who welcomed to his court all people of fair fame whether they were nobles or whether they were peasants.

One day the king was hunting in the forest with his retinue and they lost their way, so that they were obliged to take refuge in a hermit's hut. It was the hermitage of Saint Corentin.

King Grallon had often heard of this holy man and was glad to have been led to his abode. But the servants of the king looked askance at the saint's poor hut and said to themselves that they would get only prayers for supper. The saint guessed their thoughts, for he understood much of what passed in the minds of men.

So he asked the king if he and his servants would accept light food and drink and, as they had eaten nothing since cockcrow, the king gladly accepted.

Saint Corentin called the king's cupbearer and his cook and told them to prepare a meal. He led them to a spring nearby where he filled the cupbearer's golden jar with water. A small fish was swimming in the water, and this the saintly hermit took and, cutting off a bit, gave it to the cook. Then he told the cook and bearer to hasten and lay the cloth for the king and all his retinue.

The cupbearer and the cook burst out laughing and asked Saint Corentin if he took the courtiers of the king for beggars since he dared to offer them naught but bones of fish and frogs' wine. But the saint answered them that heaven would provide. Grumblingly the two laid the cloth when, to their vast surprise, Saint Corentin's promise was fulfilled. The water in the golden jar changed into wine as sweet as honey and as warm as fire, and the piece of fish became so multiplied that it would have satisfied twice as many guests. as the king had in all his retinue.

The cupbearer and the cook related to the king this miracle, and showed him also another marvel: the fish that the saint had cut in two was swimming in the brook as whole as if the saint's knife had never touched it! When the king saw this he was seized with wonderment and said to the hermit:

"Man of God, your place is not here, for your Master and mine has forbidden us to hide our light under a bushel. You must leave this hermitage and come to my city of Quimper where you will be consecrated bishop. My own palace shall be your dwelling place and the town itself will I give into your keeping."

And so it was that the king gave up Quimper unto the holy hermit and went to live in the city of Ker-Is.

Now King Grallon had an only daughter, the Princess Ahez. But she was not upright like her father. Indeed her conduct was so evil that in order to be out of her father's sight she had left his court and had gone to the city of Ker-Is where the king now followed her.

Ker-Is was so magnificent and beautiful that when men of the olden times wished to praise the French folks' mighty town—now Paris—they could think of words none other than Par-Is, that is to say the equal of Is.

Stately Is was built below the level of the sea and was protected by dykes, the doors of which were opened at certain hours to allow the water to pass in and out. The wicked princess always carried the silver keys of these doors hanging around her neck, and that is why people called her the Princess Ahez which means the Key-bearer.

As she was a powerful magician she had decorated the town with things too difficult for man's hands to make. All the elves around had come thither at her command to build the dykes and forge the gates. They had covered the palace with metal that gleamed with golden light and had surrounded the gardens with balustrades that shone like polished steel. It was the elves, too, that looked after the princess' stables. The stalls were resplendent with red, white or black marble according to the color of the horses.

These obedient elves were also keepers of the harbor. There they fed the sea dragons. For the Princess Ahez had the sea beasts in her power also. Indeed, she had given these monsters to the inhabitants of Ker-Is. They rode the dragons beyond the seas and carried back rare stuffs and treasures, and with the monsters' might they drove away the ships of enemies. Thus the townsfolk had become so rich that they measured their grain with cups of gold.

But alas, wealth had made them wicked and hardhearted. The poor and the helpless were driven from the town. The church was so forsaken that the beadle had lost the key; nettles were growing on the threshold and swallows nested in the joints of the door. The townsfolk spent their days and nights in taverns, theatres, and ballrooms, knowing no business more absorbing than the losing of their souls.

In wickedness Ahez was the moving spirit. Day and night there was feasting in her palace. Knights and princes came from far countries drawn by the fame of the princess' beauty. And many a handsome man did the wicked Ahez slay. She gave each one, when he arrived at the palace, a magic mask which made him invisible, but when he left her the enchanted mask would tighten and strangle him. A black man would appear and, taking the body would fling it across his horse like a sack of corn. He would then ride to a high precipice and throw the corpse into the sea. And this is true, for even now you can hear their souls moaning in the abyss.

Saint Corentin, who knew all that was happening at Ker-Is, had warned King Grallon that punishment would follow his daughter's deeds. But the king was powerless. He lived alone, forsaken by everyone save a few faithful servants, like a grandfather who has handed over his possessions to his children.

As for the Princess Ahez she paid no attention to the Saint's predictions.

Now one evening when there were riotous festivities in the palace, a powerful prince was announced. He had come from the ends of the earth to see Ahez. He towered head and shoulders above all the people and his beard was so immense that his eyes were all but hidden. They shone like stars upon a sea of blackness.

He addressed compliments to the princess in verse. No bard from all that countryside could match his rhyme nor wit. The princess and her guests were astonished. Yet what amazed and pleased them more was to discover how much cleverer in wickedness this bearded stranger was than they themselves. He knew not only all the wickedness that men have practised since the beginning of the world, but he seemed to know all

62

that they would invent till the end of time. The princess and her courtiers had to acknowledge their master, and they resolved to take lessons from the bearded stranger. They did not know that he was Old Nick alarmed for his own power by the increasing wickedness of the princess.

He first offered to teach them a new dance. It was none other than the dance of the seven deadly sins, and for this he called in his piper, a dwarf dressed in goatskin. Hardly had the dwarf begun to pipe than the princess and her friends were seized with a frenzy of delight and began to whirl in a mad dance. The bearded stranger took advantage of this confusion to snatch the silver keys, unnoticed, from the princess' neck and vanish from the ballroom.

While this was happening the king was sitting alone in the seclusion of his own domain. He was in a vaulted and shadowed room seated near the hearth where a dull fire smouldered. His heart was full of anguish and he wept. Suddenly the door opened and Saint Corentin appeared. A halo glowed about his head and in his hand was a bishop's staff. He was walking in a cloud of incense.

"Rise up, great king," said he to Grallon. "Take anything precious you still possess and flee. For this accursed city has given itself into the power of the Demon."

King Grallon, terrified, rose up at once. Seizing his most precious treasures he hurriedly left his castle, mounted his black charger and set forth for the city's gates. The saint went with him, gliding through the air.

As they passed before the massive dyke they heard a rumbling of water. They saw the bearded stranger, who had now resumed his demon shape, busily opening the locks with the silver keys he had snatched from the Princess Ahez. The sea was already rushing in, and the towering waves were dashing, even now, over the white roofs of the city. The dragons chained in the harbor bellowed with terror, for animals know when death is drawing near. The king longed to cry a warning to his people but Saint Corentin urged him onward in his flight. His horse passed swiftly through the streets and squares pursued by the angry sea. Always were the steed's hind legs in water no matter how furiously he leaped.

As they passed the entrance to the Princess Ahez' palace she appeared on the steps, her hair floating out behind her. She rushed after her father and seized his charger's rein. The good horse stopped so that the princess might mount behind the king, up to whose knees the flood had already risen.

"Help! Help! Corentin!" the king shouted in despair.

"Throw off the load of sin you have behind you!" called back the saint.

The king, who despite his daughter's wickedness had for her a father's love, knew not what to do. Meanwhile the waves rose swiftly higher. But Corentin came quickly and touched the princess' shoulder with his bishop's staff. Immediately she rolled off the horse into the sea, and was sucked down into an abyss of waters called ever after the Pit of Ahez.

When the king's horse was delivered from his burden he leaped forward and with one bound reached the rock of Carrec. Here, even to this day, upon the granite may be seen the mark of the black steed's hoofs. Thus was the king's life saved.

King Grallon fell upon his knees and thanked God for his deliverance. Then, standing, he looked toward Ker-Is, the once beautiful city. There, where had been stately houses and glittering palaces was now a bay upon whose waters were reflected the stars. Then the king turned and beheld on the horizon, standing on the last remnant of the submerged dykes, the bearded stranger triumphantly shaking the silver keys.

THE CHANGELING

Mariannik and little Loik

MARIANNIK and her husband lived in a thatched cottage. It was hidden in a lonely heath like a bird's nest in a tree. In the summer the thatch was covered with flowers and matched the heath itself. in winter it looked like a rough, furry coat thrown over the cottage's shoulders to keep it warm.

Within, the cottage danced in firelight. Here was an ancient linen press on which were carved curious figures. In the corner stood the box bed, its sliding doors cut in fanciful lace patterns. The chest, the table, and the benches were polished till they shone in the light from the burning logs. Near the fireplace was the cradle, also of carved wood, and in the cradle was Mariannik's and her husband's treasure, the darling of the cottage, Loik, their little son.

One day Loik was sleeping peacefully, the fire was crackling merrily, and the cat seated on the warm hearthstone was purring and washing her face. Mariannik got up and looked out of the window.

"The sun is shining now," she said, "but I know it is going to rain, because pussy is washing behind her ears; that is a sure sign. I'll go and fetch a bucket of water before the rain muddies the spring."

She kissed Loik and set out for the fountain where she filled her bucket. As she was coming back she saw a tiny, crested bird singing on a hawthorn bush, and this is what he sang:

"Mariannik, be quick, be quick,
For in the cradle is no Loik."

"You silly bird!" exclaimed Mariannik, "Loik cannot walk," but all the same with a flutter at her heart she hurried across the heath to the cottage.

She opened the door and felt at once that something terrible had happened. The fire had gone out. The cat's back was bristling. She hastened to the cradle where, instead of seeing Loik's round and rosy face, Oh, lack-a-day! she beheld a hideous dwarf with a dark and spotted face. He had a huge and gaping mouth; his hands and feet were evil, threatening, jagged claws.

"Merciful heavens!" cried Mariannik. "Who, are you? What have you done with my blessed child?"

The dwarf answered never a word, but grinned a wicked grin.

When Mariannik's husband came in from the fields he found her weeping, the baby gone, the dwarf howling, the cat spitting, and the cottage cold.

They took counsel together and decided that Mariannik must go back to the hawthorn bush where the bird had sung to her.

So back she went and when she got there, sure enough, there sat the crested bird perched on a swinging twig.

"Little bird, little bird," cried Mariannik, "my Loik is lost, and a wicked dwarf is in his cradle. Pray tell me what to do."

"Mariannik, Mariannik," chirped the little bird, "your Loik is not lost, he has been stolen by the Queen of the Dwarfs. Before he can be rescued you must make the changeling speak. Now mark well what I say. Go home and in an eggshell prepare a meal for ten strong ploughmen. Then will the dwarf demand of you what you are doing. Quickly, Mariannik, seize him and beat him with all your strength. Beat him till he screams for help. His mother, the Queen of the Dwarfs, will come and give you back your Loik."

So Mariannik hurried to the cottage, and without a word she took an eggshell and in it began to prepare a meal for ten strong ploughmen.

"What are you doing, mother, what are you doing?" shrieked the ugly dwarf, sitting upright in the cradle.

"What am I doing, hideous creature, what am I doing? I am preparing a meal for ten ploughmen in an eggshell."

"A meal for ten ploughmen in an eggshell, mother? I saw the egg before I saw the white hen. I saw the acorn before I saw the oak tree. I saw the tree in the enchanted woods, but I never saw a sight such as this."

"You have seen too many things, thou hideous one. Thou son of evil, I have you now!" And Mariannik beat him with all the power of her arm.

"Help! help!" screeched the creature, calling for his mother, the Queen of all the Dwarfs.

"Mariannik, Mariannik! Forbear from beating of my son," cried a shrill, excited voice. "Behold I give you Loik!"

Breathless, Mariannik stopped. The yells had ceased. She looked at the cradle in amazement. The ugly dwarf had disappeared and Loik, her beloved child Loik, was there again. As Mariannik bent over him to kiss him he stretched out his arms to her and said:

"Mother, mother, dear little mother, what a long sleep I have had."

THE FOSTER BROTHER

How swift thy steed, my love, my love

How swift thy steed, my love, my love

THE loveliest girl of noble race in all the country round was a maiden
of eighteen summers whose name was Gwennola. The old lord of the
manor, her father, was dead. Her two sisters, likewise, as well as her own
sweet mother had passed beyond this world; all of her family were gone
except, alas, her stepmother.

It was sad to see the lovely Gwennola, so sweet and winsome a maid,
weeping bitterly on the doorstep of the manor house. Her eyes were

fixed on the sea watching for the return of her foster brother's ship. This hope was her only comfort, and she had waited long. Her eyes never left the far horizon seeking for the sail of her foster brother's vessel. It was six years now since he had sailed away from home.

Her stepmother called to her sharply, "Out upon you, thou idle, starveling! Go, away to the marsh and call the cattle home. Shall I give you food and drink for sitting alone and idle?"

She was hard and cruel, this stepmother. Every morning in the cold winter she woke Gwennola before daybreak and bade her build the fire and sweep the hearth. And then perforce was the maiden sent to stumble through the dark and draw water from the spring in the black dwarf's brook. Her stepmother made her carry a cracked jug and a leaking bucket.

One morning when Gwennola went to the spring in the first pale light of dawn, she found the water muddied. By the brook's brim there stood a steed and on his back there sat a glistening knight. The knight spoke to her. "Long life to you, fair maid. Are you betrothed?" he said.

She was a child and timid, and she replied, "Sir, I know not."

"Are you betrothed? I beg you, tell me," again the horseman asked.

"Heaven bless you, Sir Knight, I am not betrothed as yet." Gwennola answered tremblingly.

"Then take my golden ring, and tell your stepmother you are betrothed to a knight returned from Nantes. Tell her there has been at Nantes a battle, and the knight's young squire is slain, and he himself is wounded by a sword thrust. But say to her that in three weeks and three days he will come to the manor and marry the fair Gwennola."

They said farewell; she hastened home. And when she looked at the ring, it was the ring her foster brother had worn on his left hand.

One week, two weeks, three weeks went by and the young knight had not yet come home.

Then said the stepmother to Gwennola, "You must get married, and I have decided what to do. I have found, daughter, just the husband that you need."

"Have mercy, stepmother! I desire no other husband than my foster brother who will be home again. He has given me my wedding ring, and in three days he will come and carry me hence."

"Be silent about your golden wedding ring!" commanded the cruel woman. "Else I will take a stick to teach you how to talk to me. Whether you wish it or not it is Cracked Joe, the stable groom, that you are going to marry."

"You wish me to marry Cracked Joe the stable groom! Oh, fie upon you!" cried the fair Gwennola, "I should die of grief . . . Oh, mother, my own dear mother, if you were but in this world today!"

"Go and weep in the stable yard," jeered the cruel stepmother. "Sob and cry as much as you like. No matter how many antics you perform, in three days the wedded wife of Cracked Joe you shall be."

And even while they talked the white-haired sexton was on his way about the countryside ringing his plaintive bell. He carried tidings of death.

"Pray for the soul of a noble knight," he called, "For he was a kind, great-hearted man. He was mortally wounded near Nantes by a cruel sword thrust. Tomorrow at sunset the funeral watch will begin, and the next morning we shall bear him from the white church to the tomb."

At the wedding feast one guest said to another, "You are going home early!"

"Am I going home early? Yes, that am I indeed. The wedding feast is not over, the dancing has not begun. But I cannot hide the pity my heart feels for the bride, nor the horror I have for the cowherd, Cracked Joe, who is seated beside her in the manor."

Around the poor maid, Gwennola, everyone was shedding tears, even the parish priest. And in the church that morning everyone had wept, young and old, except the stepmother.

When they had come back to the manor house the more gayly the bagpipers played or the more her friends tried to comfort her the more the heart of the lovely Gwennola was torn. They led her to the table, to the highest seat, but neither a sip of water nor a mouthful of bread would she take. They wished to lead her to the bridal chamber but she threw away her ring and tore off her bridal wreath.

Then she fled away from the house, her fair locks flowing out behind her. And none knew whither she had gone.

The lights were out, all were asleep in the manor house, but the poor maid who was in hiding was shivering with fever. At length she heard a noise, as if someone were approaching.

"Who is there?" she asked.

"Nola, it is I, thy beloved."

"Is it you? Ah, really you? Yes, it is you, my own, my darling," Gwennola cried.

She ran out from her hiding place and climbed behind the knight on his white steed. She twined her pale arms around him, she put her cheek against his cold armor.

"How swiftly we are riding, my love, my love!" the maiden said. "Me seemeth we have ridden a hundred leagues. How happy I am with you, with you, with you! Never has my heart beat so joyously as now. Is my mother's house far distant? Fain would I reach it."

"Hold tightly, beloved, soon we shall be there."

The night owl sped hooting before them, and the wild beasts of the forest fled frightened by the sound of the horse's hoofs echoing strangely on the wind of night.

"How lithe is thy steed and how bright thine armor! How tall thou art grown, love of my heart! Is mine own mother's manor far from here?" asked Gwennola.

"Hold tightly, my dear, my sweet, soon shall we be there."

"Thy heart is of ice, thy hair is damp, thy hand is chill as the winter's wind. I fear thou art acold," the maiden said.

"Hold tightly, my dear, my sweet, it is not far. Hearest thou not the heavenly music they are playing so joyfully for our wedding day?"

Hardly had the knight thus spoken when his white steed stopped. The animal was trembling from mane to hoof. Was it fear or ecstasy that resounded in his neigh?

The knight and maid were on an island where folk were merrymaking, where youths and damsels frolicked beneath fragrant, bounteous trees. The trees were laden with bright apples. Behind them the sun was rising o'er the mountains. A brook was sparkling joyously by. Its waters were the water of life. Behold, were this bubbling brook but quaffed it brought again to life and youth those souls who had left behind on earth forever their weary, mortal bodies.

Gwennola's mother and two sisters were among these lovely men and maidens. And around them was naught but happiness, songs and joyful cries.

The next morning when the sun arose the weeping wedding guests bore the spotless body of little Gwennola from her hiding place to her last bed in the tomb.

THE HUNCHBACK AND THE ELVES

Guilcher on the haunted heath

Guilcher on the haunted heath

IN the parish of Plaudren in Brittany there used to be a certain heath on which, amidst rows of towering stones, there was a village of elves. Here the mischievous imps danced every night and if you dared to venture on their domain they were sure to drag you into their carousal. They would make you whirl around and around in their fairy ring until the cock crew. That is why no one dared go near the heath after nightfall.

However, there was a man who braved the moorland. His name was Guilcher. One evening he was coming home with his wife from a field, weary after ploughing, when he decided to take a short-cut across the haunted heath. As it was early he hoped that the elves had not begun their dance. But when Guilcher and his wife were in the middle of that waste land he saw the elves scattered among the huge stones, like sparrows in a corn field. He was about to turn back when he heard the horns of the wood elves echoing behind him. Guilcher's legs began to shake.

"By Saint Anne, we are done for!" he groaned to his wife. "The singing elves and the underground elves have joined in with the dancing imps to keep the ball going all night long. They will make us dance till daybreak and I know my poor heart will burst."

And in truth troops of fairy creatures came bounding from all sides and surrounded Guilcher and his wife. But when the elves noticed the old wooden fork, for cleaning the plough, that Guilcher had in his hand they drew back.

Then they all began to sing together:

"Let them be, let them be,
A fork has he, can't you see?
Let them be, let them be,
The oaken fork has he."

Then Guilcher understood that the forked piece of oak he had in his hand was a magic defense against the mischievous fairy folk. So with his wife he walked straight through their midst, and the elves lifted not a finger to molest him.

This was welcome news indeed for all folk of that countryside, and from that time forward all anyone had to do when he wanted to cross the heath in the evening unmolested was to carry a bit of forked oak wood.

But Guilcher was not satisfied to have done everyone a good turn, he was still curious about the elves. Now you must know that Guilcher was

75

a merry, gay-tempered man, but the poor fellow was a hunchback. Yes, he had a hump just between his two shoulders that he would gladly have sold for ready money.

One evening his longing to see the elves got the better of him, so he took his oaken fork and set out for the heath. The elves saw him coming and ran to him shouting, "It is Guilcher! See, 'tis Guilcher!"

"Yes, little men, it is Guilcher," answered the cheery hunchback. "I have come to pay you a call."

"Welcome, welcome," cried the elves. "Won't you dance with us?"

"Please excuse me, kind friends," replied Guilcher, "but you are too long-winded for a poor human with a load between his shoulders."

"We will stop when you like," shouted all the elves.

"Will you promise to stop when I say the word?" asked Guilcher, who wanted to try the dance just out of curiosity, and most of all to be able to boast about it afterwards.

"We promise, we promise," they all cried in one voice.

So the hunchback took his place in the fairy ring and the elves began to whirl around and around, singing their usual song, which was nothing more than:

"Mon-day, Tues-day, Wednes-day."

After a few moments Guilcher stopped to catch his breath and said to the dwarfs: "In spite of the respect that I have for you little gentlemen I must say that your song and your dance have precious little variety. You end too soon in the week. I shall add a bit to your lay."

"Do it, do it!" cried the elves.

So the hunchback took up the words and sang in a deep voice:

"Mon-day, Tues-day, Wednes-day,
Thurs-day, Fri-day, Satur-day."

A shout went up from the dwarfs.

"Hurrah! hurrah!" they yelled, surrounding Guilcher. "You are a lusty singer and a fine dancer too. Sing it again, sing it again," they all cried.

The hunchback repeated his verse while the elves whirled round him, wild with joy. At last they ceased, and crowding once more around Guilcher all chimed out together:

"What would you like? Make a wish, and we will give you what your heart desires. Which will you have, wealth or beauty?"

"Well," replied the hunchback, "since you wish to make me a present, and since you let me choose it myself, I shall ask you for only one thing: take off what I have between my two shoulders and make me as straight as a staff on a steeple."

"That we will! that we will!" exclaimed the dwarfs. "Come hither, come hither," and catching hold of Guilcher, they tossed him from one to the other as though he had been a mere cork from a bottle until each imp had had his fling. Then they dropped Guilcher on the ground, giddy, breathless, and wonderful to see! without his hump. Guilcher now was tall and handsome, straight as the staff on a steeple, and unless you had been his own true mother you never would have known him.

You can imagine everyone's surprise when he appeared again at home. Not one of all his neighbors knew that he was Guilcher. Even his wife was not sure whether she ought to take him in. Guilcher was obliged to tell her exactly how many coifs she had in her linen press and the color of her four pairs of stockings before she was really sure that he was her husband.

Then everybody wanted to know how he had gotten rid of his hump. But Guilcher was afraid to tell. If, thought he, the neighbors knew he was friendly with the elves, each time an ox went astray or a goat was lost they would expect him to find it. So he held fast to his secret.

Now there lived in the parish a squinting tailor whom people called Perr the Stutterer, because he stammered. He was a gloomy miser and never laughed or sang. He ate rye bread so coarse that in it you could see the very husks and straw. What is more he was a usurer and lent money at so high a rate that he had brought about the ruin of many a poor man in that country.

Now Guilcher the hunchback owed Perr the Stutterer five crowns, and he could not manage to pay it back. One day the miser went to Guilcher and said he would grant him a week's delay on condition that Guilcher would tell how he had gotten rid of his hump. And so Guilcher was obliged to tell his secret. Perr then wished to hear again and yet again the words that Guilcher had added to the elves' refrain and then the tailor grumblingly remarked that he would give Guilcher, as he had promised, a week to pay back the five crowns.

But all Perr had just heard had aroused his miser's passion. The tale kept buzzing in his head and he made up his mind to go that very evening to the heath and dance with the elves and so, too, have the choice of wealth or beauty.

As soon as the moon arose squinting Perr set out for the heath with a bit of forked oak wood in his hand. No sooner had the elves espied him than running out to meet him, they invited him to join their reel. Perr consented on condition they would let him stop when he was tired just as they had granted Guilcher. So he began dancing in the fairy ring while the imps burst into their song.

"Wait a moment," shouted the tailor, suddenly inspired, "I want to add something to your song too."

"Yes, do!" cried all the elves, as they repeated their refrain:

"Mon-day, Tues-day, Wednes-day,
Thurs-day, Fri-day, Satur-day."

Then they stopped and waited for Perr to add his word. Perr very much excited began to stutter:

"And Su . . . Su . . . Su . . . Sun . . . de . . . de . . . day . . . te . . . te . . . te . . ." stuttered the tailor, trying very hard to say it.

"But what comes after?" cried the elves.

"Su . . . Su . . . Su . . . Sun . . . de . . . de . . . day . . . te . . . te . . . Sunday too!" he stammered out at last.

The elves' ring broke up and they all ran about as if bereft of their wits.

Perr was frightened and stood with his mouth wide open. At last the sea of little black heads became calmer, they surrounded Perr and a thousand voices shouted at once:

"Make a wish! make a wish!"

Perr's courage came back with a bound.

"Gui . . . Gui . . . Guilcher could che . . . che . . . choose either wealth or be . . . be . . . beauty?" he managed to question.

"Yes, yes! Guilcher chose beauty and left wealth," the elves cried back.

"I am go . . . go . . . going to . . . to . . . choose what Gui . . . Gui . . . Guilcher left!" stuttered the miserly Perr.

"Very well, tailor," shouted the voices, "come along, come along."

Perr was delighted. The dwarfs caught him up and tossed him to and fro even as they had tossed Guilcher. They threw him bounding from hand to hand all around the ring. But, alas for Perr, when he fell on the ground, there, between his two shoulders was what Guilcher had left—a hump!

So Perr went home, his heart welling with black rage, swearing to avenge himself on Guilcher. And when the week was up and the time had come for Guilcher to pay the five crowns Perr with threats informed him that if he did not pay he would have to sell at once all of Guilcher's household goods. It was in vain the other pleaded. The, new hunchback turned a deaf ear to the poor man's supplications and told Guilcher that on the morrow he would put up his furniture, his pig, and tools at auction and that too, on his very doorstep.

Guilcher's wife began to cry that they were in disgrace and that there was nothing left for him to do but to beg from door to door, with his wallet on his back and his staff in hand. She wailed it was not worth while for Guilcher to have become so straight and handsome if he were to be a beggar.

Guilcher felt very sad. He was angry with himself now for not having preferred wealth when he was free to choose. He would gladly have taken back his hump if it could have been filled with golden crowns or even silver coins. So he made up his mind to return to the heath and try his luck once more with the elves.

Guilcher went that very evening. The elves welcomed him with joyous cries and made a place for him in the ring. They were singing the song to which Guilcher had added a line. But there were still no words to finish it. This seemed very dull to Guilcher. He brought up in the mad whirl and all but breathless panted out, "Your ditty seems somewhat like a butcher's dog, it limps."

"That is true, that is true, add to it," cried all the elves at once. And they continued in their shrill voices:

> "Mon-day, Tues-day, Wednes-day,
> Thurs-day, Fri-day, Satur-day."

They paused waiting for Guilcher to finish. He quickly lifted up his voice and added:

> "Sunday is the next day,
> And so the week has slipped away."

A thousand cries rose from the heath, and in a moment the elves were everywhere. They came out of the tufts of grass, the flowering broom, the crevasses of the rocks. They leaped about among the heather singing:

"At last the hunchback breaks the charm,
He sets us free and safe from harm."

"What does all this mean?" asked Guilcher astonished.

"It means," answered the king of the elves, "that we were under a spell to remain among men and dance every night on the heath until a Christian chanced to end our lay. You added a line and we hoped the tailor would finish the song but he stopped just before his line was finished and that is why we punished him. You at last have ended the verse and so the spell is broken. We are free to go back to our kingdom under the earth."

"If that be so, and I have done you a good turn," said Guilcher, "will you help me out of some sore trouble?

"What do you want?" they asked at once.

"Not very much, only five crowns to pay that miserly tailor," answered Guilcher.

"Take our bags! take our bags!" cried the elves.

And they threw down at Guilcher's feet the plump wallets of brownish linen that were strapped upon their backs. Guilcher picked up as many as he could carry and hurried home.

"Light the pine torch," he called to his wife as he came in the door, "and close the shutters so that our neighbors cannot see us. For I have money enough to buy up three of the richest parishes in all of Brittany!"

He threw the plump bags upon the table and began to open them. But alas, he had counted the price of butter before he had bought the cow. For the wallets had in them only sand, dead leaves, and a pair of scissors.

Guilcher uttered a heartbroken cry so that his wife, who was bolting the door, turned quickly around and asked him what was the matter.

Then Guilcher poured out to her his tale of where he had gotten the wallets and all about what had happened to him upon the heath.

"Heaven help us!" cried the good woman. "The elves have been making sport of you."

"Alas! So I see," answered Guilcher, shaking his head sadly.

"Unfortunate man, see what comes of touching bags that have belonged to those accursed beings!" cried his wife.

"Indeed I thought they would have something better in them than sand and dead leaves," sighed Guilcher.

"Nothing good can come out of what is good for nothing," retorted his wife. "What you have there will bring us evil fortune for sure and certain. Pray heaven I have a drop of holy water!"

She rushed to the bedside and took a little stoup which had holy water in it, and ran back to the table. Hardly had she sprinkled a drop upon the bags than the dead leaves were turned into golden coins, the sand into diamonds, and the scissors into the most magnificent of clothes.

Thus was the spell broken. The wealth that the magic of the elves had hidden from Christian folk assumed its true form again.

The very next morning Guilcher paid the five crowns to Perr the Stutterer. And the next day he gave to all the poor in his parish a bushel of corn and six ells of linen. Then he and his wife set out for Josselin where they bought a house well unto their liking. There they lived happily for many years and had a lot of children who are all fine gentlemen today.

THE FOUR GIFTS

The dame peered at Téphany

IF I had three hundred crowns a year, I should go and live at Quimper, where is the finest church in all Cornouailles and where all the houses have weather-cocks; if I had two hundred crowns a year, I should go and live at Carhaix, for its moorlands and game, but if I had only one hundred crowns, I should settle down at Pont-Aven, for it is there you find an abundance of everything. At Pont-Aven, butter costs but the price of milk at Quimper, a fowl what you pay for a Quimper egg. That is why at Pont-Aven you see fine farms, where you have home-cured bacon three times a week and even shepherd-lads have as much homemade bread as they can eat.

It was in one of such estates that Azénor Bourhis lived; she toiled from dawn till night, keeping her farm as though she had been born a man, and owning fields and produce enough to pay for two sons' schooling. But in place of sons Azénor had one niece who earned more than her keep, so that each day's savings were added to the day's before. Thus the old dame's purse grew fat before her very eyes.

Now, savings too easily earned bring evil in their train. If you store up corn, rats come into the barn, and if you hoard up crowns, miserliness grips the heart. Old Azénor had gotten to the point of caring only about wealth, and of esteeming people only like herself, who had plenty of money in their pockets. So she was angry when she saw Dénès, a farm laborer from Plover, having private talks with her niece.

One day when Azénor again had seen the two together she called to Téphany in a rasping tone:

"Are you not ashamed to be chattering with that beggar, when you can find many a rich lad hereabouts who would be glad to buy you a silver ring?"

"Dénès is a skillful farmer and as upright as the hills," replied the maiden. "One of these days he will find a farm to let, big enough to bring up little children on it."

"And you would like to be their mother?" burst out Azénor wrathfully. "By my purse strings! I would rather see you at the bottom of our well, than the wife of that good-for-nothing. No! No! No one shall say I have brought up my sister's child only to see her marry a man whose whole possessions could go into his tobacco-pouch!"

"What does money matter when you have health and the good saints know your intentions are of the best?" answered Téphany gently.

"What does money matter!" retorted Azénor, horrorstruck. "Do you then despise the goods that heaven gives us! Since it is so, you impertinent

84

baggage, I forbid you to speak again to Dénès, and if I catch him on our lands I shall ask the Rector to blame you publicly on Sunday!"

"Oh! you would not truly do so!" cried Téphany quite terrified.

"As sure as there is a Paradise waiting for us all, I will!" flared back the angry dame. "In the meantime, away to the brook with you and wash the linen and put it to dry on the hawthorn hedge, for ever since you've listened to the wind that blows from Plover town, all your work has been forgotten, and both your arms are worth no more than a one-armed man's five fingers."

With which bitter words Azénor pointed to the scrubbing board and ordered Téphany to her task. The girl obeyed, but her heart was welling with grief and resentment.

"Crabbed age is harder than the stone stoop of our farm," she brooded. "Yes, a hundred times as hard, for the rain, falling drop by drop, wears away the stone but tears cannot soften old folks' stubbornness. Heaven knows my meetings with Dénès were my only joy. He never taught me anything but beautiful songs, and talked to me only about what we should do when we were married in our little farm,—he looking after the land, and the mangers. Is it wrong to give each other courage and hope? God would never have created marriage if it were a sin to think of one's own wedding! Ah! cruel, cruel aunt to tear me from my Dénès!"

So thinking, Téphany reached the brook. As she was putting down her tub of linen on the flat, white stones that marked the washing-place, she saw a wizened woman, not of that parish, who was leaning on a hawthorn wand. In spite of her trouble, Téphany greeted her, calling her "Aunt," according to the ways of Old Breton courtesy. Young folk had warm hearts in those days of long ago.

"Are you resting under the cool willow tree, Aunt?" she asked.

"You have to rest where best you may, when the sky is your only roof," replied the shrivelled woman in a quavery voice.

"Are you then so forlorn?" inquired Téphany pitifully, "and have you no relations to give you welcome in their home?"

"All have gone to heaven," continued the crone, "and my only home is kind hearts."

The maiden took the piece of homemade bread and the slice of bacon which Azénor had given her, wrapped up in a bit of clean linen, and offered it to the beggar woman. The dame had a hungry look.

"Take this, poor Aunt," said Téphany. "Today at least, with this good bread you will have a Christian dinner. In your prayers, remember my dear parents who have died."

The dame took the bread and peered at Téphany.

"Those who help are worthy to be helped," she remarked. "Your eyes are red because your aunt Azénor has forbidden you to talk to your lad from Plover,—but I shall give you the means of seeing him once a day."

"You will!" cried the girl, dumfounded that this old dame should know so much about her.

"Take this brass pin," resumed the crone. "Each time you prick it into your collar Mother Bourhis will feel compelled to leave the farmhouse and go into the field to count her cabbages. As long as the pin is in its place you will be free and your aunt will come back only when the pin lies once more in its sheath."

Having pronounced these words, the beggar woman rose, waved her hand and disappeared.

Téphany stood thunderstruck. It was certain that the wrinkled dame had been a saint or fairy. The girl went home quite decided to try what the pin could do.

The next day at about the time that Dénès usually arrived Téphany placed the brass pin in her collar. Immediately Azénor took her wooden shoes and went out into the garden, where she fell to counting the cabbages. From the garden, she went to the orchard, from the orchard, to the other fields, so that the lassie had plenty of time to talk with the lad from Plover.

It was the same the next day, and every day for week following week. As soon as the pin came from its sheath, Téphany's aunt would trot off to her cabbages and begin to calculate again and yet again the number of the big ones, the little ones, the smooth ones or the curly. Who would not have a pin like this! At first Dénès was delighted, but as week followed week he became less eager for his talks with Téphany. He had taught her all the songs he knew. He had gone over his plans again and again and now he was obliged to wonder what he was going to say to her, and to get it ready beforehand, as a preacher prepares his sermon. So he came later and went away earlier. At length days arrived when he did not come at all, and the waiting Téphany twiddled her pin in vain.

Alas, poor Téphany!

She felt her lover's heart becoming cold and she was sadder now than in the days before she had the magic pin.

There came an evening when Téphany, having waited uselessly for her beloved, took her pitcher and went alone to the spring, her heart heavy with sorrow. As she drew near, she beheld again the wizened woman, who had given her the pin. When the crone saw Téphany she began to laugh and addressed her in a squeaky voice:

"Ah! Ah! my fine lady does not care about being able to talk to her beloved Dénès at any time in the day?"

"Alas," sighed Téphany, "I had to see him to keep his heart in love with me, but now habit has made my society less pleasant. Ah! Aunt! since you gave me the means of seeing him every day, you ought to have given me the wit to hold him."

"Is that then what my lassie wants?" asked the aged woman. "So be it. Here is a feather. It comes from the wing of the oldest of the eagles, and no one knows how old he is. When my fair lady hides it in her hair, she will be as knowing as the will-o'-the-wisp himself."

Téphany, blushing with pleasure, took the feather and the next day, before Dénès' visit, she slipped it under the blue ribbon of her coif. It seemed instantly as if the sun had risen in her mind. She found knowledge that men take all of a lifetime to acquire was hers. A wealth, too, of other matters filled her brain which learned men know not at all. For to man's wisdom was added woman's wit. So Dénès was astonished at her flow of knowledge; she invented poetry and knew more songs than all the singers of Scaër, and repeated all the gossip of the neighborhood that on baking-days was going round from house to house.

The young man came back the next day and the days that followed, and Téphany had always something fresh to tell him. Dénès had never met a man nor woman half so witty, but it was not long before he felt himself a bit uneasy in his mind. Téphany could not help wearing her feather for other folk as well as Dénès and all over the countryside tongues began to wag about her songs and clever speeches.

"She's a bad lot," folk said of her. "The man who marries her will be led along for all the world like a bridled horse."

The lad from Plover began repeating the same prediction to himself, and as he had always thought it better to hold the bridle than to wear it, Téphany's jokes no longer made him laugh so heartily.

One day when he was going to a dance on a new threshing floor, the girl did her brightest to prevent him, but Dénès, who did not intend to be directed by her, would not listen to her reasons and laughed at her request.

"Ah! I see why you are so anxious to go to the, new threshing floor," explained Téphany in a temper. "Azilicz will be there."

Azilicz was the prettiest girl in all the countryside and, as even all her best friends said, the vainest.

"It is certain Azilicz will be there," said Dénès, who was pleased to make his best-beloved jealous, "and a man would go a wearier way than that to see a maid so winsome."

"Then go where your heart bids you," cried Téphany, and she flounced into the farmhouse without listening to another word.

She sat down upon the hearthstone, overwhelmed with grief, and, tearing from her hair her magic feather, sobbed aloud with bitterness.

"Of what use is wit since men turn toward beauty as flies turn toward the sun! Ah! old fairy Aunt, what I needed was not to be the most learned, but the most beautiful of damsels."

"Then be the most beautiful," replied a voice close to her ear.

Téphany turned breathless, and behold! beside her stood the wrinkled crone with the hawthorn wand. The dame went on: "Take this necklace, and while you have it round your neck you will be to other women as the queen of flowers is to the wild blossoms of the meadows." Truly here was a necklace indeed!

Téphany uttered a cry of joy. She quickly donned the necklace, hastened to her looking-glass and gasped delighted. Never had been seen in all the land of Brittany a maid so flowerlike as she.

She determined to test immediately her beauty upon Dénès so, putting on her richest costume, her woollen stockings and buckled shoes, she set out for the threshing floor. When she reached the cross-roads, she met a young lord in a coach.

"By our Lady," he cried, leaping out beside her, "I did not know there was such a lovely creature in all the four corners of the land, and if I lose my soul for it, you shall bear my name."

But Téphany replied:

"Go your way, my lord, go your way; I am only a poor peasant girl, used to winnowing, milking and harvesting."

"And I will make a lady of you!" exclaimed the lord, seizing her hand and drawing her toward his coach.

The girl drew back.

"I want only to be betrothed to Dénès, the ploughman of Plover," she cried, alarmed. But the young lord laughed. He ordered his servants to lay hands on Téphany and to lift her into his coach, which done they drove away as quickly as the horses could gallop. Amidst clouds of dust and a clattering of hoofs they reached the young lord's castle, which was of rock, roofed with slate, as are all the great nobles' houses. Her captor imprisoned Téphany in a vast and vaulted room, closed it with three bolted doors and placed guards to keep watch upon her. But scarcely had the young lord withdrawn than Téphany with sudden inspiration drew forth her pin of brass. At once her watchers hastened to the garden to count the cabbages. She then placed the feather in her hair and with her wits discovered, hidden in the panelling, a fourth door through which she fled. Soon she gained the brushwood through which she plunged as a wild creature that hears the hounds hot in pursuit.

She panted on until night began to fall, then she found herself beside a convent at whose grated door she knocked and asked for shelter. The doorkeeper, when she beheld Téphany, shook her head.

"Nay, nay," she growled out surlily, "this is no place for smartly dressed girls who go about alone at night." And she clapped the door shut and dropped the clanging bolts into place.

Téphany stumbled on and on and came at length to a farm where lights were twinkling. Here again she stopped to ask for succor. At the door a boisterous group of farm-lads greeted her. They all cried out at Téphany's dazzling beauty, each one demanding that he have her for his wife. This quickly led to quarrelling, and the quarrelling in turn to fighting, so that frightened Téphany turned to flee. But all the lads ran after her. Suddenly remembering her necklace, she snatched it from her neck and threw it on a sow. At once the spell was broken that drew the lads to her. Her pursuers now pursued the pig, which grunted off in terror, and all vanished in the dark.

Téphany stumbled on her way and at last footsore, and sad at heart, she reached her aunt Azénor's farm.

So fraught with danger and with hardship had been the gift of beauty that Téphany found herself once more forming wishes. "Heaven forgive me!" she whispered to herself, "what I ought to have asked for, was neither the liberty of seeing Dénès every day, for he wearies of it, nor a sharp wit, for it frightens him away, nor beauty, for it brings troubles and distrust; I ought to have asked for wealth, which makes you master of yourself and all the world beside. Ah! if I dared ask the fairy for one thing more, I should be wiser than I was before!"

"Take your heart's wish," said the beggar woman's voice at Téphany's ear. "If you feel in your right-hand pocket, you will find a silver box. Rub your eyes with the pomade and you will have a treasure in yourself."

The girl felt quickly in her pocket, found the box, opened it and had just begun to rub her eyes, when Azénor Bourhis suddenly appeared.

For some time past, Azénor had lost long days in counting cabbages, and as she saw all work behindhand in the farm, she was on the watch for someone on whom to vent her temper. When she beheld her niece sitting idle, she exploded in a burst of wrath:

"Aha, and that's the way you work, while I am slaving in the fields! Behold why ruin is in the house! Naught do you with shiftless fingers but steal the bread of your own relation!"

Azénor's anger was like milk that boils upon the fire, as soon as it boils it overflows the pot. From reproaches Azénor went to threats and then from threats to blows. Téphany, at the irate woman's onslaught burst into sobs and you can guess what was her amazement, when she beheld each tear become a round and shining pearl.

Old Mother Bourhis, uttering a cry of admiration, began to snatch them up.

Dénès too, arriving, stared with eyes like saucers.

"Pearls! pearls!" he cried out in excitement.

"It's a fortune for us," babbled Azénor who continued to sweep them up in handfuls. "No one else must know about this, Dénès. Weep on, Téphany, weep on!"

She held out her apron and Dénès his hat. He was thinking only about the pearls, and had forgotten they were his sweetheart's tears. Thus can mere sight of wealth befuddle wits of men!

"Alack, alack the tears are stopping!" Azénor now explained. "By all the saints, Téphany if I had luck like yours I would out-weep the very rains from Heaven! Shall we beat her, Dénès, and bring her sobs again?"

"No, no," broke in Dénès, "we mustn't wear her out the first time. As for me I shall start for town at once and find out what each pearl is worth."

"And I shall go with you!" cried Azénor, and the two hastily left the house.

Téphany, alone at last, clasped her hands upon her heart. In anguish she raised her eyes to Heaven, then dropped them to the dark chimney corner where suddenly she saw again the wrinkled beggar woman. The crone's regard was bent upon her with a strange and mocking smile. The girl started, then with a gesture of despair, held out toward the fairy the pin, the feather and the box of ointment.

"Take them back!" Téphany cried. "Woe to people who are not content with gifts that God has granted. Give other girls wit, beauty, wealth; I wish to be again the simple-hearted girl I was."

The smile broadened on the old crone's face, "That is right, Téphany," said she, "you have learned much through your ordeal. I was sent to give you this lesson, and now you will live happily for ever after."

At these words, the beggar woman was changed into a sparkling fairy. Light flooded the cottage and she disappeared in a cloud, sweetly scented with violets and rose.

Téphany forgave Dénès for having wished to sell her tears, and as they were both no longer hard to please, they were as happy as it is possible to be upon this earth. She married the lad from Plover and he was always the devoted husband that her heart had longed to have.

THE MAGIC ROCKS AND THE BEGGAR

Wells filled with Precious Stones

Wells filled with Precious Stones

IN Brittany near the sea there is a village called Plouhinec. It is surrounded by moors with here and there a grove of fir trees. There is not enough grass in the whole parish to rear an ox for the butcher nor enough bran to fatten a little pig.

But if the folk there have neither corn nor cattle they have more stones than you would need to build a town. For just outside the village there is a big stretch of heather where long ago the Korrigans, a race of elves who lived in ancient Brittany, planted two rows of tall rocks which look for all the world like an avenue, except that they lead nowhere.

Near there on the banks of the river there once lived a man named Marzin. He was rich for the place, that is to say, he could salt down a pig every day, eat as much black bread as he wanted, and buy a pair of wooden shoes every Palm Sunday.

So everyone said he was proud and haughty. He had refused his sister Rozen's hand to several ardent lovers, who earned their daily bread by the sweat of their brows.

Among the suitors for the hand of Rozen was a youth named Bernez. He was a steadfast toiler, upright as the day is long, but unfortunately he possessed nothing in the world save his industry.

Bernez had known Rozen since she was a tiny girl and when she grew up his love had grown up, too. So you can quite understand that Marzin's refusal to consider him as worthy of his sister's hand nearly broke poor Bernez' heart. Rozen, however, was still permitted to welcome Bernez on the farm.

Now one Christmas eve there was a storm and people were unable to get to midnight mass. So Marzin invited all the field-hands and several neighbors to his farm. Bernez was among them. The master of the house, to show his generosity, had planned to treat them all to a supper of pig's pudding, and a whole-meal pudding sweetened with honey. All eyes were fixed on the open fire where the supper was cooking, all, that is, except those of Bernez, who kept gazing at his darling Rozen.

Now just as Bernez was drawing the benches up to the table and Rozen had stuck the wooden spoons in a circle in the huge pasty basin, the door was pushed open and an ugly old man stepped into the room.

He was a beggar, a strange man, who had never put his foot inside a church door, and the God-fearing people were afraid of him. They accused him of placing a curse on the cattle and making the corn blacken in the ear. Some folk even went so far as to say he could turn himself into a werewolf.

94

However, as he wore a beggar's habit, farmer Marzin let him come near the fire, gave him a three-legged stool to sit upon and the same share of the food as the invited guests.

When the old beggar, whom folks called a wizard, had finished his meal, he asked where he could sleep. Marzin opened the door of the stable where there was only a skinny donkey and a scraggy ox. The beggar went into the stable, lay down between them to get their warmth and put his head on a sack filled with chopped heather.

Now you must remember that it was Christmas eve, and just as the beggar was about to fall asleep, midnight struck, that mysterious hour when animals of the stable are said to talk like men.

The old donkey shook his long ears and turned toward the scraggy ox.

"Well, cousin, how have you been getting on since Christmas a year ago when I last spoke to you?" he asked in a friendly voice.

"It is not worth while for us to have a gift of speech on Christmas eve on account of our ancestors having been present at the birth of the Holy Babe," the ox answered crossly, "if our only hearer is an old-good-for-nothing like this beggar."

"You are very proud, my lord of Lowing Castle," said the donkey, laughing. "But I know how to be satisfied with what I have. Anyhow can you not see that the old beggar is asleep?"

"All his witchcraft doesn't make him any the richer," the ox said, "and then when he dies he will go to a nice warm place without much profit to himself. It is strange that his chum, Old Nick, has not told him of the good luck to be had near here merely for the asking."

"What luck is that?" said the donkey.

"Well," sniffed the ox, "didn't you know that once every hundred years, and the time is drawing near, for it is on this New Year's eve, a strange thing happens? The great rocks just outside the village leave their places and go down to the river to drink. Then it is that the treasures they guard beneath them are laid bare."

"Yes, yes, I remember now," answered the donkey, "but the rocks return so quickly that they catch you and grind you into powder. Folks say that the only way to avoid their fury is to hunt a branch of verbena and bind it with a five-leaved clover. This is magic against all disaster."

"But there is another condition harder to fulfill," said the ox. "The treasures that you find will fall into dust unless in return a human soul be sacrificed. Yes, you must cause a human death if you wish to enjoy the wealth of Plouhinec." When he had said this both the animals became silent.

Now all this time the beggar had been listening to their conversation, hardly daring to breathe.

"Ah, dear beasts," he thought to himself, "you have made me rich. And you can wager your last wisp of hay that this old beggar will not go below for nothing!"

And so the wizard fell asleep. But at crack of dawn, he hastened out into the country, his eyes all eagerness to find verbena and the five-leaved clover. Well-nigh endlessly he looked, up and down, here and there, hunting inland where the air is mild and plants keep green all the year round. At last, on New Year's eve, he came back to the little town of Plouhinec. His hands were clutching as though at treasure. His face bore a striking resemblance to that of a weasel that has found its way into a dove-cote.

As he was walking across the heath to the place where the huge rocks stand, he saw Bernez. Bernez, with a pointed hammer in his hand, was chipping away at one of the largest rocks.

"Well, well," mocked the wizard, "are you trying to hollow a house out of this great stone pillar?"

"No," said Bernez quietly, "but as I am out of work just now I thought I would carve a cross on one of these accursed rocks. Perhaps it will be agreeable to Providence, and possibly I shall some day be rewarded."

"You have a request to make then?" asked the old beggar slyly.

"Every Christian wishes the salvation of his soul," answered the lad.

"Have you nothing else to ask for?" whispered the beggar.

"Ah, so you know that too!" exclaimed poor Bernez.

"Well, after all it is no sin. I love the dearest maid of all Brittany and long to go before the priest with her. But alas, her brother wants for her a husband who can count out more silver coins than I have lucky pennies."

"What would you say if I could put you in the way of earning more gold coins than the maiden's brother has silver?" murmured the wizard.

"You!" exclaimed Bernez.

"Yes, I!"

"But what will you want in return?" inquired Bernez.

"Only a prayer when you say yours," answered the wicked wizard.

"Then tell me what to do!" cried Bernez, letting his hammer fall. "I am willing to risk a score of deaths. For I should rather die than not win Rozen."

When the wizard saw Bernez was so eager he explained that the next night at the stroke of twelve the great rocks would go down to the river to drink, leaving their treasures uncovered, But the crafty beggar did not tell Bernez how to avoid being crushed when the stones returned to their places.

The lad suspected nothing. He thought he had but to be brave and swift.

"As there is a Heaven above us I shall do what you say, old man," said he. "And there will always be a pint of my blood at your service for what you have told me. Let me finish the cross that I am cutting on this rock," he continued, picking up his hammer, "and when the appointed hour arrives I shall meet you on the edge of the moor."

Bernez kept his word and was at the meeting place one hour before midnight. The beggar was already there. He had three knapsacks, one in each hand, and another hanging around his neck ready to be filled with treasure.

"Well," said the beggar to the young man, "sit down beside me and tell me what you will do when you have as much silver, gold and precious stones as you can dream of," said he.

Bernez stretched out on the heather. "When I have as much as I like," said he, "I shall give my sweet Rozen everything she wishes, linen and silk, white bread and oranges."

"And what will you do when you have as much gold as you like?" the wizard asked.

"When I have as much gold as I like," the lad answered, "I shall make Rozen's family rich, and all their friends and all their friends, too, to the limits of the parish!"

"And what will you do when you have many precious stones?" went on the wizard, laughing up his sleeve.

"Then," cried Bernez, "I shall make everyone rich and happy, and I shall declare it to be of Rozen's doing!"

While they were talking, an hour slipped by. From the distant village came the stroke of midnight. Scarcely had the last note sounded when there was convulsion on the heath and in the starlight the huge rocks could be seen, leaping from their beds, tumbling headlong towards the river to quench a century's thirst. They rushed down the hillside tearing up the soil and reeling like a throng of drunken giants. They then disappeared into the darkness.

The beggar leapt through the heather, followed by Bernez, to the place where the rocks had been. There, where they stood, two wells were glittering, filled up to their brims with gold, silver and precious stones.

Bernez uttered a cry of delight, but the beggar began to cram his wallets in the wildest haste, all the while listening for the return of the rocks, his ear turned toward the river.

He had just finished stuffing his knapsacks and Bernez had managed to pocket a few gold pieces for himself when a dull rumbling was heard, which swelled rapidly to thunder.

The rocks had finished drinking and were coming to their places. Tumultuously they plunged forward, faster than man can run, crushing everything before them.

When Bernez saw the rocks upon them he could not move: he cried aloud, "We are done for!"

"*You* are!" sneered the wizard, "but this will save me," and he clasped tightly in his hand the verbena and the clover. "You must die in order for this wealth to be mine!" shouted the wizard. "Give up your dear Rozen and think about your sins!"

While the beggar was shouting the rocks rushed headlong on him but he held up his magic leaves and the huge stones stopped with a violent jerk; then passing to the right and to the left, they rushed upon Bernez.

Bernez saw that all was over. He fell on his knees and closed his eyes. The mightiest rock of all was leading. Suddenly as it reached the kneeling Bernez, a strange thing happened. The huge stone stopped, closing up the way, standing before Bernez like a barrier to protect him.

Bernez opened his eyes. Upon the mighty stone he beheld the cross that he had carved. The stone now could do no harm to a Christian. There it remained motionless before the young man till all the others had resumed their places, and then on it went, tumbling toward its own. It came upon the beggar by this time bent double with his laden bags.

The beggar held up the magic plants but the rock was carved with a cross and in consequence was no longer in the power of evil spells. It hurled itself upon the wizard and crushed him into powder.

As for Bernez, he picked himself up and slung upon his back the wizard's bags of silver, gold and precious stones, and trudged off for home with them.

And so he married pretty Rozen after all. Together they lived as happily as both their hearts. desired, and brought up as many children as has a jenny-wren in a brood.

THE COUNTRY BUMPKIN AND
THE HOBGOBLIN

Jegu loved Barbaïk with all his heart

Jegu Loved Barbaïk with all his heart

BEHIND the town of Morlaix there is a beautiful glen which shelters many fine farms where cattle are bred and corn is grown. Here, long ago, one of the largest of these farms was tenanted by a good man whose name was Jalm. His only child, Barbaïk, was a girl whose beauty was the boast of the countryside. Her face was lovely as a June rose, and her figure had all the charm of glowing youth and grace. And she was considered the best dancer and the daintiest heiress in all that broad country.

On Sundays, when she went to St. Mathew's church, she wore an embroidered cap, and a kerchief with large flowers on it. And she had five skirts, worn one above the other. Some of the old wives shook their heads as she went by and asked if she had sold the black hen to Old Nick and had thus gotten by uncanny means both beauty and fine clothes.

But Barbaïk, who really was rather vain, cared nothing for what they said so long as she knew that she was the best dressed girl in the parish and the one after whom the lads ran. For that is what always happens. The hearts of young men are like wisps of straw hanging on a bush, and the beauty of maids is like the wind that carries them along in its train.

Among Barbaïk's suitors there was one who loved her more than all the others. He was her father's farm hand, Jegu, a steadfast and upright Christian. But, alas, he was as rough as a Northerner and as ugly as a tailor. Barbaïk would not listen to him in spite of all his merits. She always laughed and spoke of him as "the country bumpkin."

But Jegu loved her with all his heart. He bore all her insults and allowed himself to be badly treated by the girl who made joy and grief for him.

Now one evening as he was bringing his horses back from the pasture he stopped at a quiet pool to let them drink. He stood near the smaller horse, his head fallen on his breast. From time to time he would heave a sigh, for he was thinking of Barbaïk. Suddenly a voice spoke to him, seemingly coming from the reeds that grew by the edge of the pool.

"Jegu, why are you grieving so?" the voice inquired. "You are not done for yet."

The ploughman was very much astonished you may be sure. He raised his head and looking about him asked, "Who are you?"

"I am the hobgoblin of the pool," the voice replied.

"But I cannot see you," replied Jegu.

"Look carefully into the reeds and you will see me," the voice answered. "I am disguised as a green frog. I can take any form I wish. And I can make myself invisible."

"Can you show yourself to me in the form that your race usually takes?" asked Jegu.

"I can if you wish," said the voice.

As it spoke a green frog hopped onto the back of one of the horses. It rested there a moment and then suddenly changed into a beautiful little gnome. He was dressed in apple green and was wearing shiny gaiters for all the world like a leather dealer.

Jegu felt some alarm and drew back a step or two. "Why are you afraid, Jegu?" said the green gnome with a smile. "I will not do you harm; on the contrary, I wish to help you."

"But why do you wish to help me?" asked the ploughman rather suspiciously.

"On account of a good turn you did me last winter," said the hobgoblin. "Did you know that the elves of the white corn country declared war on our race?" continued the hobgoblin. "They accused us of helping mankind. And we were obliged to turn ourselves into animals in order to hide. Since then we often take these forms to amuse ourselves. That is how I came to know you last winter."

"How was that?" asked Jegu.

"Do you remember one day when you were ploughing the alder-field you found a poor little redbreast caught in a snare?" asked the hobgoblin.

"Yes," answered Jegu, "and I even remember what I said: it was 'You do not eat the corn of Christian folk, so take your flight, bird of Heaven.'"

"Well I was that bird!" the hobgoblin continued. "And at that time I swore to be your friend. And I am going to prove it to you now by helping you to marry Barbaïk."

"Oh, dear little hobgoblin, if you succeed in doing that I shall never refuse you anything, except my soul!" Jegu replied eagerly.

"Let us arrange it all," the gnome said, "and in a few months' time you will be the master of the farm and the husband of Barbaïk."

"And how will you manage that?" asked the youth.

"You will know that later on," replied the hobgoblin. "Go on smoking your pipe; eat, drink, and do not worry."

Jegu said that would be easy enough and that he could obey the pixie's orders. Then Jegu thanked the little green man and took off his bat just as he did to the mayor or the priest. After which he led his horses home.

The next day was Sunday, but Barbaïk got up at the usual early hour, for it was her duty to look after the stables.

Imagine her surprise when she found that some one had already filled the mangers and milked the cows. She remembered that she had said, on the evening before to Jegu, that she wanted to be ready so as to go to a dance at the Pardon of St. Nicolas. So, when she found the cows milked and the mangers filled, she thought it was Jegu who had done it, and she thanked him. He answered gruffly that he did not know what she meant, but the way he said it made her think all the more it had been be who had done the work.

After that some kind turn was done for her every day. Never had the stable been so clean nor the cows so plump. Every morning and evening Barbaïk found her jars full of milk, and a pound of butter freshly churned and decorated with a blackberry leaf lying on the table. This meant that now she did not have to get up till broad daylight, just in time to tidy up the house and get the breakfast.

Sometimes even this work was done for her. One morning when she arose she found the house swept and clean, the furniture polished, the soup boiling on the fire, and the bread cut up and put in the bowls; so that all she had to do was to walk as far as the barn door and call the men in from the field.

She imagined it was a kind attention of Jegu's, and she could not help thinking that he would be a very convenient husband for a woman fond of taking things easy, even if he were a country bumpkin.

In fact the heiress had only to express a wish in Jegu's hearing and it would be fulfilled at once. If the wind were too cold or the sun too hot and she was afraid of spoiling her complexion, she would say, "I should like to see my churn clean and in its place, and my water jugs full of fresh water and covered with fresh linen." Then she would go off to have a chat with her neighbor and when she came back there would be her churns and water jugs standing on the cool flag just as she wished them.

If the rye bread were too heavy to knead, and the oven slow in heating she had only to murmur, "Oh! I wish my fifteen pound loaves were in a row on the bread shelf!" and behold! when next she came into the kitchen, the loaves would be ready for her, beautifully baked.

Again, if the market seemed too far away, and the road so full of ruts that driving was hard, she had only to say the evening before so that Jegu could hear her, "If I were only back home from Morlaix with my milk jar empty, my butter dish in the bottom of it, a pound of ripe cherries on the wooden plate and a silver piece in my apron pocket!" Next morning she would get up and find the empty milk jar with the butter dish in the bottom of it, the pound of ripe cherries on the wooden plate, and a glittering silver piece in her apron pocket.

These happenings did not stop here. For if she wanted to send word to another girl to go with her to Morlaix to buy a few yards of ribbon, or if she wanted to know at what time the procession was to set out from the church she had only to say the word and it would happen at once. And it seemed always to be Jegu who was the cause of it.

So she began to imagine that she could not live without the country bumpkin. She needed him for work and for play; he was her faithful dog and her guardian angel, she thought.

At last the hobgoblin advised Jegu to ask for her hand and this time Barbaïk gave heed to his wooing. She thought him far from handsome, and clumsy as a lover, but as a husband he would do very well. He would manage all the work and she could sleep late as did the town lady, and wear fine clothes and spend her time on her neighbor's doorstep with her hands folded in her lap. And she would continue to dance at all the Pardons. She imagined that Jegu would be like the horse obliged to drag the cart, while she would be the proud driver perched high on her bundle of hay, making her nag jog along to the flick of her whip. So while Jegu talked she pictured to herself the rosy future. Then she answered him as a well-brought-up heiress is bound to make answer to her suitor. She said she would do as her father wished. But she knew that Jalm would consent, for her father had said more than once that Jegu would make a fine manager for the farm.

So, in the course of the next month, they were married.

It seemed as though the old farmer were only waiting for that event before taking his leave of this world, for he died a few days after the wedding, leaving the farm to the young couple.

It was a heavy burden for Jegu, but the good little hobgoblin came to his assistance. The gnome did the ploughing, and he accomplished as much work as four ordinary hired men. It was the gnome who kept the tools and the harness in repair, and he always told Jegu the best time for sowing the grain and for the reaping.

If Jegu had any work that must be finished at once the little green gnome would quickly bring his friends to help. All the pixies would come either with pitchforks, or hoes, or reaping-hooks on their shoulders, and the work would be done in no time.

When Jegu was short of horses the hobgoblin would tell him to go to one of the pixie towns out on the heath and to say, "Little friends, lend me a team of horses and everything they need for ploughing," and the team would appear in less time than takes the telling.

And, most surprising of all, the hobgoblin of the pool asked in payment for all these deeds only as much pudding each day as would fill the old dipper.

Jegu was grateful to the hobgoblin and loved him as his own son. But Barbaïk hated the gaitered imp. She had her own reasons for that. For beginning the very day after her marriage, to her astonishment, no one helped her any longer with her work. And when she complained to Jegu about it he did not seem to understand her.

But the gnome, who was near, overheard her lament and burst out laughing. He then confessed to her with grins that he had done all the kind deeds in order to make her agree to marry Jegu. Now, however, he said he had other things to busy him and she would have to look after the house herself.

So disappointed and surprised was Jalm's daughter that she was filled with awful wrath against the hobgoblin. How dared the creature treat her thus?

Every morning now Barbaïk had to get up before the sun to milk her cows or go to market. And evenings up she had to sit till midnight churning butter. She was embittered with the imp who had deceived her and had led her to look forward to an idle, care-free life. And she waxed yet angrier and angrier when she gazed on poor Jegu's red face, squinting eyes, and coarse hair.

"No, no, wicked elf," she vowed to herself, "never will I forgive you for having made me marry a country bumpkin! But for you I should still be the heiress, courted by the lads. I should still go to dances and all my suitors would bring me cherries, hazelnuts and the good things of the seas, and I should hear them tell me that I am the prettiest girl in all the countryside. But now I must accept nothing save from my clumsy husband. I must please only him! O wicked, spiteful elf!"

Yet wonder of wonders! One day the gnome did offer to help her. She was invited to a wedding and as all the horses of the farm were ploughing in the fields she asked the hobgoblin for a steed. He told her to go to the pixies' town and ask for exactly what she wanted.

So Barbaïk went to the pixies' town on the heath and thinking that she was asking properly, she said, "Little elves, little elves, lend me a black horse, with eyes, mouth and ears, and with a bridle and a saddle."

No sooner asked than granted. The horse she wished stood instantly before her. She mounted him and set out for the wedding. But soon she began to notice that everyone laughed as she passed by.

"Look, look," cried each. one to his neighbor, "the farmer's wife has sold her horse's tail!"

Barbaïk looked around quickly, and sure enough, her horse had no tail! She had forgotten to mention one when she told the pixies what she wished. They had taken her at her word and had given her just what she had asked for.

Barbaïk was sorely vexed and tried to ride on quickly, but the horse would not go faster, and she had to put up with all the jokes of the passers-by.

By the time she reached home that evening, instead of being grateful for the pixies' generosity, she was angrier than ever with the little man in green. She accused him of having played a crafty trick upon her. She made up her mind to punish him.

It was not long before spring came. Now spring is the birthday time of all gnomes, elves, and fairies, and the little hobgoblin asked Jegu if he might be permitted to invite his friends, the other little hobgoblins, to come and spend the night in the hospitable barn, for he wanted to give them supper and a dance. Of course Jegu could not refuse the gnome this pleasure, so he asked Barbaïk to put her best tablecloth on the barn floor, and to serve buttered rolls, all the day's milk, and as many pancakes as she could make in one morning.

To Jegu's surprise Barbaïk did not object. She made the pancakes, prepared the milk and baked the rolls and then, at nightfall, took them to the barn and arranged them for the goblins' feast.

But she did something else that Jegu had not asked for. She put the red hot cinders she had just taken from the fire all around the tablecloth in the places where the pixies would sit down. So when the hobgoblin and his friends arrived for the merrymaking they sat on the hot coals and burned themselves most painfully. Up they all jumped and fled with shrill cries of dismay and pain.

But in a twinkling they were back with jugs of water and after having put out the fiery coals they began dancing around the barn singing in angry voices:

"Oh! naughty, idle Barbaïk
Has played on us a horrid trick,
So from the country we shall flee
And leave her to her misery."

And they vanished from the farm that very evening, never to return.

From that night forward Jegu and Barbaïk had all the labor of the farm to do themselves for there were no kind elves to help them, nor to bring their wishes true. But some folks said Jegu still had ten pixies to work for him, pixies that were not invisible: his eight fingers and his two thumbs!

THE WASP, THE WINGED NEEDLE AND THE SPIDER

Three Angels dazzling with light.

Three Angels dazzling with light.

Long ago there lived, at Leon in Brittany, two young noblemen so rich and so handsome that their own mother could discover no defect in them. Their names were Tonyk and Mylie.

Mylie, the elder, was sixteen, but Tonyk was only fourteen. Both were well educated, and Tonyk was of a pious disposition. He was always ready to help the poor and to forgive evil. Money stuck to his fingers no more than anger lingered in his heart.

Mylie, on the contrary, liked to give to people only what was strictly due them. He was a bargainer. It is sad to say, too, that if anyone offended him he never failed to take his vengeance if he could.

As their father was called to Heaven when they were still wearing petticoats, their mother brought them up. But now that they were older she thought it was time to send them to their uncle who lived in one of Brittany's farthest corners. Their father's brother would give them good advice as well as all his property later on when he, too, should be summoned into Paradise.

One fine morning their mother gave each of the brothers a new hat, silver-buckled shoes, a violet cloak, and a purse full of money. She told them it was now time to set out for their uncle's castle.

The two boys began their journey, delighted to think that at last they were to see something of the world. Their horses travelled quickly, and in a few days' time they were in another dukedom, in a country where grew trees and corn of different sorts than those at home.

Now it happened one morning as they were riding along the road that they saw a poor woman seated near a wayside cross, her face hidden in her apron.

Tonyk reined in his horse at once and asked, "Why do you grieve, good dame?"

The beggar woman sobbed and said, "I have lost my son who was all I had in the world, and now I am left on the charity of the Christian folk."

The boy's heart was touched, but Mylie who had moved on a few paces called back in mocking tones:

"Are you going to believe the story of the first old, sniffy, crone you come across? She is sitting there just to coax money out of people's purses."

"Brother, be quiet!" exclaimed Tonyk. "Your unkind words are making her weep more than ever. Do you not notice that she is about the age of our own mother?"

Then bending over the beggar Tonyk gave her his purse, saying, "I can give you only this small aid. But I shall pray that you be comforted in your grief."

The tattered beggar accepted the purse and said, "Since the young lord wishes to help the poor he will not refuse to accept this little gift in return: it is a walnut containing a wasp whose sting is made from a diamond."

Tonyk took the walnut and, thanking the old dame, went on his way with Mylie.

The two brothers soon reached the outskirts of a forest. There they saw a little child dressed only in thin rags. He was rummaging in a hollow tree and singing to himself a song more mournful than the music of the mass for the dead. He stopped every now and then to rub his ice-cold hands, chanting as he did so, "I am cold! I am cold!" and then again, "The wind is cold!"

Tears came to Tonyk's eyes, and he said to his brother, "Mylie, see how that little child is suffering from the wind."

"Oh, he is just the chilly sort, I suppose," answered Mylie, "I do not think the wind is cold."

"That is because you have on a velvet doublet, a cloth coat, and on top of all that your violet cloak, while this little child's clothes are but the winds themselves."

"You are right," laughed Mylie, "but he is only a peasant."

"Alas, brother," said Tonyk, "when I think that you might have been born in his place, my heart bleeds. I cannot bear to see him suffer."

So saying, he alighted from his horse and, calling the lad to him, asked what he was doing.

"I am looking for winged needles," said the child. "They are sleeping in the hollow trees."

"And what do you intend to do with your winged needles?" inquired Tonyk.

"When I have a great many I shall sell them in the town, and then I shall buy such warm clothes that it will seem to me that the sun is always shining."

"Have you found many?" asked the young lord.

"Only one," replied the child, showing Tonyk a tiny reed cage in which he had put a small blue dragon fly.

"Very well, I shall buy it," said Tonyk, throwing his own violet cloak around the child. "Wrap yourself in that, poor lad. And when you say your prayers, pray for my brother Mylie and for our mother."

The two brothers journeyed on again. At first Tonyk suffered from the wind and sadly missed his cloak. But after they had passed through the forest a softer breeze began to blow and the sun shone warmly.

At length they came to a meadow where there was a spring and near the spring was seated a bent and aged man with a beggar's knapsack upon his shoulder. As soon as he saw the two riders he called to them in an entreating voice.

Tonyk went to him. "What do you want, father?" he asked, taking off his hat out of respect for the beggar's snowy locks.

"Alas, my dear young lords," replied the beggar, "see my hair, how white it is! How wrinkled my cheeks! I am old and weak and my feet can carry me no longer. I shall die here if one of you will not consent to sell me his horse."

"Sell you one of our horses, old beggar!" cried Mylie disdainfully. "How can you pay for it?"

"Do you see this?" asked the beggar, holding up a hollow acorn for the brothers to behold. "It contains a spider that can weave a web stronger than steel chains. Give me one of your horses and in exchange I'll give you the spider in the acorn."

The elder brother burst out laughing.

"Did you ever hear of such stuff, Tonyk?" he asked, turning to his brother.

"The poor can offer only what they have," answered the younger brother gently.

Then dismounting Tonyk said to the beggar, "I shall give you my horse, old man. Not on account of the hollow acorn that you offer in exchange, but in memory of the saints in Heaven. Take the horse as if he were your own, and thank Heaven that we crossed your path today."

The old man murmured a blessing and, helped by the lad, he mounted the horse and disappeared across the meadow.

But Mylie could not forgive his brother this last act of generosity.

"You fool!" he burst out angrily. "Look at the state you are in now through your own silliness! No doubt You thought that when you gave everything away I would let you take half of my money, half of my cloak, and ride on my horse. But do not hope for that. I wish the lesson to be brought home to you. You will be more careful in the future when you realize the inconvenience of extravagance."

"Yes, this is indeed a lesson, brother," answered Tonyk gently. "And I shall take it to heart. But I have never thought of sharing your money, or your horse, or your cloak. Go your way and trouble not about me, and may the angels guard you."

Mylie said nothing in answer but rode off as quickly as his horse could trot whilst the younger brother continued his journey on foot.

Riding thus, and followed by his brother trudging in the dust, Mylie came to a gorge between two lofty mountains. It was called the Accursed Gully because a wicked ogre lived there, who was always on the alert for travellers who chanced to pass. He was as blind as a stone, but his hearing was so sharp that he could detect an earthworm hollowing out its hole.. His servants were two eagles he had trained, for he was a powerful magician. When he heard travellers approaching he would send the eagles to capture them. That is why people, when travelling through the gorge, carried their shoes in their hands, scarcely daring to draw breath.

But Mylie knew nothing of the ogre. Into the gorge he clattered, as bold as brass. At the ring of the horse's hoofs the giant awoke.

"Come hither, come hither, my fleet eagles," cried he. "Where do you tarry?"

The red eagle and the white eagle flapped quickly into the cave.

"My supper is riding by!" exclaimed the ogre. "Away and fetch it!

The two eagles darted off and plunged into the depths of the ravine. They seized Mylie by his velvet cloak and bore him aloft to the ogre's dwelling.

At that moment Tonyk reached the opening of the gorge, just in time to see his brother carried off by the two great birds. He pursued them shouting, but the eagles and Mylie soared into the clouds that covered the highest peak and were swallowed up from view.

The lad stood overcome with grief, staring at the rock that rose straight upward like a wall. Then he fell on his knees and prayed:

"O, Creator of the world, save my brother Mylie!"

At once he heard three shrill voices near him calling, "Let us help you! Let us help you!"

Tonyk turned around surprised.

"Who spoke to me?" he asked.

"We are in your jacket pocket," the voices answered.

Tonyk put his hand in his pocket and pulled out the acorn, the walnut, and the reed cage which held the dragon fly.

"Can you save Mylie?" he asked in astonishment.

"Yes! Yes! Yes!" piped the tiny voices, each in a different key.

"But how will you manage that, you poor little nothings?" asked Tonyk.

"Open our prisons and you will see," they answered.

The boy did as they wished. The spider came out of the acorn and fell to weaving a web as shining and as strong as steel. Then he climbed on the back of the dragon fly, who had just come out of his little cage, and together they rose gently in the air. And as they rose the spider continued to weave his web. The threads were so spun that they formed a lengthening ladder. Tonyk at once began to climb, following the spider and the dragon fly, until he reached the top of the mountain. Then the wasp who had been shut up in the walnut shell flew before them. Thus they came to the ogre's cave.

It was a cavernous grotto hollowed out of the rock and looked to be as high as a church. In the middle sat the blind ogre. He was swaying to and fro like a poplar tree in a gale, singing a wild song of his own invention, and cutting slices of bacon with which to baste Mylie. Poor Mylie lay at the ogre's feet with legs and arms trussed like a chicken ready for the boiling. The two eagles were near by. One was winding up the turnspit and the other was blowing the fire with a mighty bellows.

The ogre was making such a noise with his song and he was so busy slicing the bacon that he did not hear Tonyk and his three little servants enter. But the red eagle noticed the boy, flew at him, and was about to catch him up in his claws when the wasp came to the rescue. It darted at the eagle and pierced his eyes with its diamond sting. The white eagle flew to the assistance of the red eagle, but he too was blinded by the wasp.

Now it was the ogre's turn. He had stopped his song when he heard the eagles shrieking, but the wasp flew at him and began to sting him mercilessly. The ogre bellowed like a bull and threw his arms about like a windmill, but he could not catch the wasp.

At last he fell with his face to earth to escape the fiery stings. Then the spider drew near. He wove a web over the fallen giant who now lay imprisoned and motionless.

In vain the ogre called to his eagles. They were beside themselves with pain, and moreover they did not wish to free their wicked master now that he was helpless. They intended to gain freedom for themselves after their long slavery.

They flew at the steel net and began to tear at the ogre through the meshes. Each peck of a beak carried away a piece of flesh and the birds stopped only when they had gotten to the ogre's bones. Then, as a magician's flesh is poison, the eagles died upon the spot.

Meanwhile Tonyk had undone his brother's bonds, and after having kissed' him with tears of joy he led him out of the ogre's cave to the edge of the great rock.

The winged needle and the wasp appeared once more. They were harnessed to the little reed cage, but it was now turned into a coach. They invited the two brothers to take a seat within it, and when the boys had entered the spider closed the door and climbed up behind, for he was now the groom. Then the team set off as swift as the wind.

Tonyk was entranced at riding thus, high above the meadows. Over the mountains, streams and villages they flew until at last they reached their uncle's castle.

The coach rolled on to the drawbridge where the brothers saw their two horses waiting for them. On the holster of the saddle of Tonyk's horse were hanging his purse and cloak. But the purse was larger than it had been before, and the cloak was spangled with diamonds.

Tonyk in great surprise turned to ask what all this meant, but the coach had vanished, and standing there, instead of the wasp, the winged needle, and the spider were three angels dazzling with light.

The two brothers, awestruck, fell on their knees. Then one of the angels, the most handsome and most beautifully robed, approached the younger brother, and, bending over him, said:

"Fear nothing, kind heart, you were given to our care that you might go safely on your journey and now that you have reached your goal we are going back to Paradise."

Spreading their lovely wings the three angels then soared up into the heavens, leaving Tonyk and Mylie to stare after them with wonder.

YANNIK, THE FAIRY CHILD

Yannik of the Woods

THE boy Yannik lived in the woods and fields. That was long, long ago, when within the rocky shores of Finistère there were few houses or villages and even fewer cultivated pastures. In those days wild reaches of marsh and woodland were haunted by the will-o'-the-wisp, bears, and savage wolves. Then elves danced on the lonely heaths and men had strange visions.

But Yannik was growing as free as a redbreast on a branch, and, like the redbreast, wherever he went the child seemed to bring joy and fair fortune. But no song like the redbreast's carol ever came from between his lips.

When the good people of the country gave Yannik a pair of wooden shoes he smiled a radiant smile. Sometimes they gave him a ripe apple or buckwheat cakes, but a smile was his only answer. For Yannik was dumb.

Who was he? Whence came he?

None could say.

Can you tell whence the dew on the heather comes, or a ray of sunlight on the mountain tarn? Can you tell whence comes the beauty in the lark's song or the joyous leaps of the hind at the breaking of the summer dawn?

Yannik was like one of these, a presence, a light, a smile. Everyone welcomed him, but there was none who could keep him inside cottage walls. Though she had softly cradled him at nightfall, at dawn when the farmer's wife arose she saw by the ruddy firelight that Yannik's bed was empty. No one had heard him go, but on the fallen snow footsteps could be traced leading to the forest where Yannik lived with the birds and the beasts he loved.

The bears knew him and the fierce wolf thrust its confiding muzzle in Yannik's hand. The birds perched upon his shoulder and the turtle dove nestled in his bosom. All creatures of the forest guarded him as he roamed within its pathless depths.

"He is a fairy child," said the women to each other. And the men called him the Fol Goët, which means "the mad thing of the woods."

Yet when the choir sang in the tiny church Yannik always crept in and listened with so rapt a face, with clasped hands, and such shining eyes that the white-haired priest tried to persuade him to remain and learn a word or two of man's speech.

Yannik listened and smiled his radiant smile but no word ever crossed his lips until at length one summer day as he left the heat of the fields for the soft, cool shade of the church he heard the people chanting a hymn of praise. Their voices seemed to rise toward the glowing Heaven.

It was a feast day and white-robed children were singing in tones as pure and clear as heavenly harps:

"Glory! Glory! Glory!"

Yannik paused upon the door-sill, then went slowly up the aisle holding his hands before him as a blind man who gropes his way. Awed, the children hushed their song as they watched Yannik reach the foot of the high altar and, standing near the priest raise his hands and sing:

"Glory! Glory! Glory!"

From that day Yannik, the fairy child, Yannik, the mad thing of the woods, became one voice of praise. Alone in the woods, in the farmhouse kitchens, in the church, or going from door to door with the white-haired priest the child sang ever:

"Glory! Glory! Glory!"

To these words no other words were ever added.

One summer evening as the sun was setting and the peasants were coming home, weary after the day's toil, and the blue smoke was slowly rising in the air, the music of silver-toned bells filled the sky and it seemed as if the bells were pealing:

"Glory! Glory! Glory!"

"It is the song of Yannik, the dumb boy," said the people to each other, awestruck. "The Heavens are chanting it for him."

The next morning when the priest went down to the church door he saw Yannik lying across the threshold. The old man thought he was sleeping and spoke to him tenderly. But as he stooped over him he saw the boy's sweet smile frozen on his stiffened lips. The fairy child, Yannik, was dead.

And so on that very spot they built the church of Fol Goët, strong and stately as a knight's spear, but delicate as the lace coif of a fair lady.

And here it is that mothers of children whose lips are sealed, like Yannik's, bring them to be blessed in the hope that they too then will speak only words of praise and glory, and never words of hatred or of anger.

THE HAZEL SCEPTER

Sullenly the mountain opens

HOW sweetly the children are sleeping in their box-beds. The yellow dog is snoring on the warm hearth-stone, and the flickering firelight comes and goes over grandfather's ancient chair.

Midnight is striking at the church of Saint Michael of the Great Beach, midnight of this blessed Whitsuntide! It is now, good people, that you must say under your breath prayers for the souls of those you have loved. It is the hour when holy folk lay their heads on their chaff-pillows, thankful for the goods that God has given them and then fall asleep beside their slumbering children.

But Périk Skearn had no children; he was a daring young spark, and all alone in the world. He had seen the nobles of thereabouts coming to festivals of the parish, and he was envious of their horses with their silver-set bridle reins. He was jealous of their velvet coats and their silk stockings with their many-colored clocks. He longed to be as rich as the lords; to have a seat in church with a red leather cushion, and take a lovely heiress to the Pardons, sitting behind him on the pillion, one arm slipped round his waist.

That is why, this Whitsuntide, Périk was pacing up and down the Great Beach at the foot of the dunes of Saint Efflam at an hour when all good folk were sleeping in their beds. For Périk was dreaming of beautiful maidens and wealth and gold, and his longings were as many as the nests of the swallows on the wild sea-reefs.

The waves were sighing sadly on the dark horizon, the crabs were silently gnawing drowned men's bones, the wind was whistling eerily amongst the rocks as whistle the sea-robbers of the Great Beach,—but Skearn still paced up and down the sands.

He gazed upward at the cliffs, saying over and over in his mind what the bent and wrinkled beggar of the Cross of Yar had told him. In all four corners of the land of Brittany no sage was to be found with knowledge like unto this ancient beggar's. He could narrate what happened when our oldest oaks were acorns, and our hoary ravens unhatched eggs.

Now the beggar had informed Skearn that on the spot where is now the dune of Saint Efflam, was in olden times, a mighty town. Its fleets covered the sea and it was ruled over by a king whose scepter was a hazel wand with which he transformed everything as he willed. But it was decreed by Heaven that the city and the king should be punished for their crimes, so that one day, by Divine command, the shores rose up like floods of boiling water and engulfed the evil doers. Yet each year, at Whitsuntide, at the first stroke of midnight, a passage opens in the mountain and permits him who dares to enter to reach the king's abode. In the innermost chamber of this entombed palace is hanging the hazel wand which gives the holder magic power,—but he must hasten who wishes to possess it for, as the last stroke of midnight dies away, the mountain closes and will crush the unwary intruder.

Skearn had treasured the story of the bent beggar of Yar, and that is why this Whitsuntide he feverishly paced the sands of the Great Beach. At last, from Saint Michael's steeple, the first stroke of midnight sounded. Skearn started! . . . In the starlight he gazed at the granite cliff which forms the mountain wall and saw it open sullenly as might the jaws of some fell dragon awakening from slumber. Then, fixing the leathern strap of his club firmly around his wrist, he rushed forward into the jagged cliff. The cavernous interior was ghostily lighted as though by those strange rays that shine at night in graveyards. Half terrified, half eager, Skearn rushed onward through black leaping shadows and arrived at the threshold of a mighty palace, the like of which no man now living ever has beheld. Strangely it loomed within that eerie light.

The first chamber that he entered was crammed with cupboards in each of which were heaped up silver coins, as plentiful as are the grains of corn in corn-bins after the gathering, of the harvest. But Skearn knew that better things were waiting, and pressed on as the sixth stroke of midnight rang.

He came to a second chamber. Here the cupboards were overflowing with gold even as mangers overflow with flowering grass in June. Périk loved gold, but he knew still richer treasure was to be had and he hastened onward as the seventh stroke of midnight pealed.

The third room that Périk entered was full of baskets where pearls streamed like milk in the stone jars at the beginning of Spring. He longed to cram his pockets, but dashed on his way as the eighth stroke tolled.

The fourth room was lighted by coffers full of diamonds, throwing out more glory than the bonfires of dry gorse on the hillsides at Saint John's Eve. Skearn was dazzled. He paused an instant, then ran to the last room as he heard the ninth stroke ring. There he drew up suddenly, breathless with admiration. In front of the hazel scepter, hanging in a halo of light, were standing a hundred maidens, each lovely enough to melt a hundred hearts.

Each beckoned to Skearn with one fair hand whilst with the other offered a goblet that flashed as though with magic fire. Skearn, who had resisted the silver, gold, the pearls and diamonds, now stood spellbound. His heart pounded against his ribs. His gaze was fixed upon the wondrous beauty of the maidens.

The tenth stroke of midnight pealed. Skearn heard it not. The eleventh rang out and he still was motionless. And now the twelfth stroke tolled, as ominous as the gunshot of some ill-fated ship lost upon the rocks.

Périk, terrified, turned at last to flee, but it was too late. The mountain's jaws had closed once more; the hundred maidens had turned into a hundred statues of granite, and all was swallowed up in darkness.

That is how our forefathers told the story of Périk Skearn. Now you know the fate of that deluded lad who opened his heart too readily to avarice and temptation. It is wiser to be content with the blessings that good Heaven grants than to turn one's longings to unbridled dreams of treasure.

CPSIA information can be obtained
at www.ICGtesting.com
Printed in the USA
BVHW041557120319
541924BV00007BA/339/P